THE SAVOY COCKTAIL BOOK

The Savoy

Cocktail

Book

Being a
compendium of
Cocktails
Sours
Flips
Toddies
Coolers
Smashes
Daisies
Highballs
Egg Noggs
Tom Collins
Sangarees
Punches
Cobblers
Rickeys
Slings
Fizzes
Juleps, Shrubs
Frappé, Fixes and Cups

Constable London

First published in Great Britain 1930
by Constable and Company Limited
10 Orange Street London WC2H 7EG
Copyright © 1965 The Savoy Hotel Ltd
New edition 1952, Reprinted 1954, 1959
New edition, revised and reset 1965
Reprinted 1970, 1976, 1979
Paperback edition published 1985
ISBN 0 09 466230 4
Printed in Great Britain by
St Edmundsbury Press
Bury St Edmunds, Suffolk

Illustrations by William Fielding

Contents

Historical Note

Most of the people one meets in places where Cocktails grow have an idea that they know the origin of the word "Cocktail"; none of them, however, agree as to what that origin is, and in any case they are all wrong, as they always put that origin somewhere between ninety and one hundred years ago, whereas in *The Balance*, an American periodical, of May 13, 1806, we read that: "*Cock tail*, then, is a stimulating liquor, composed of *spirits* of any kind, *sugar*, *water*, and *bitters*—it is vulgarly called *bittered sling* and is supposed to be an excellent electioneering potion." This is the earliest reference to the Cocktail that has been found in print.

Historians have been misled by the word "Cocktail" into imagining that it was once in some way connected with the plumage of the domestic rooster. But this is not so. The true, authentic and incontrovertible story of the origin of the Cocktail is as follows:

Somewhere about the beginning of the last century there had been for some time very considerable friction between the American Army of the Southern States and King Axolotl VIII of Mexico. Several skirmishes and one or two battles took place, but eventually a truce was called and the King agreed to meet the American general and to discuss terms of peace with him.

The place chosen for the meeting was the King's Pavilion, and thither the American general repaired, and was accommodated with a seat on the Bench, as it were, next to King A. himself. Before opening negotiations, however, His Majesty asked the general, as one man to another, if he would like a drink, and being an American general he, of course,

7

said yes. The King gave a command and in a few moments there appeared a lady of entrancing and overwhelming beauty, bearing in her slender fingers a gold cup encrusted with rubies and containing a strange potion of her own brewing. Immediately an awed and ominous hush fell upon the assembly, for the same thought struck everyone at the same time, namely, that as there was only one cup either the King or the general would have to drink out of it first, and that the other would be bound to feel insulted. The situation was growing tense when the cupbearer seemed also to realize the difficulty, for with a sweet smile she bowed her shapely head in reverence to the assembly and drank the drink herself. Everything was saved and the conference came to a satisfactory ending, but before leaving, the general asked if he might know the name of the lady who had shown such tact. "That," proudly said the King, who had never seen the lady before, "is my daughter Coctel."

"Right," replied the general, "I will see that her name is honoured for evermore by my Army."

Coctel, of course, became Cocktail, and there you are! There exists definite unquestionable proof of the truth of this story, but no correspondence upon the subject can in any circumstances be entertained.

So much for the early history of Cocktails. Since those days the Art of the Cocktail has developed very considerably, and in the following pages you will find the essence of the Art set before you. Few people in the world could match Harry Craddock's vast knowledge of liquids of all kinds, of how to mix them, and of how to create new Cocktails for all great or state occasions, a tradition that has faithfully been continued at the Savoy ever since; so that it is in all confidence that this book is set before you—the confidence that if anything should have been omitted it is, in all probability, not worth including.

A few hints for the young mixer

Ice is nearly always an absolute essential for any Cocktail.

Never use the same ice twice.

Remember that the ingredients mix better in a shaker rather larger than is necessary to contain them.

Shake the shaker as hard as you can: don't just rock it: you are trying to wake it up, not send it to sleep!

If possible, ice your glasses before using them.

Drink your Cocktail as soon as possible. Harry Craddock was once asked what was the best way to drink a Cocktail: "*Quickly*," he replied, "while it's laughing at you!"

"If all be true that I do think
There are five reasons why men drink,
Good wine, a friend, or being dry,
Or lest we should be by-and-by,
Or any other reason why."
Henry Aldrich (1647–1710)

Cocktails

½ Gin   *Abbey Bells Cocktail*
¼ Apricot Brandy
⅛ Orange Juice
⅛ Dry Vermouth
1 dash of Grenadine
  Shake well and strain into
  cocktail glass

½ Dry Gin   *Abbey Cocktail*
¼ Lillet
¼ Orange Juice
1 dash Angostura Bitters
  Shake well and strain into
  cocktail glass

½ Absinthe   *Absinthe Cocktail*
½ water
1 dash Syrup
1 dash Angostura Bitters
  Shake well and strain into
  cocktail glass

1 liqueur glass Absinthe   *Absinthe Drip Cocktail*
  Dissolve a lump of sugar,
  using the french drip spoon,
  and fill glass with cold
  water

½ Dry Vermouth   *Addington Cocktail*
½ Sweet Vermouth
  Stir well and strain into
  medium-size glass; fill with
  soda water. Squeeze orange
  peel on top

11

Cocktails

Adonis Cocktail

1 dash Orange Bitters
⅓ Sweet Vermouth
⅔ Dry Sherry
Stir well and strain into
cocktail glass. Squeeze
orange peel on top

Affinity Cocktail

⅓ Dry Vermouth
⅓ Sweet Vermouth
⅓ Scotch Whisky
2 dashes Angostura Bitters
Stir well and strain into
cocktail glass. Squeeze
lemon peel on top

Cocktails

¾ Dry Gin *Alaska Cocktail*
¼ Yellow Chartreuse
  Shake well and strain into
  cocktail glass

1 dash Angostura Bitters *Alfonso Cocktail*
4 dashes Sweet Vermouth
¼ Dry Gin
¼ Dry Vermouth
½ Grand Marnier
  Shake well and strain into
  cocktail glass

½ Sweet Vermouth *Alice Mine Cocktail*
½ Kummel
2 dashes Scotch Whisky
  Shake well and strain into
  cocktail glass

1 dash Lemon Juice *Allen Cocktail*
⅓ Maraschino
⅔ Gin
  Shake well and strain into
  cocktail glass

½ Dry Gin *Allies Cocktail*
½ Dry Vermouth
2 dashes Kummel
  Shake well and strain into
  cocktail glass

Cocktails

Almond Cocktail
(6 people)

Slightly warm 2 glasses of Gin Add a teaspoonful of powdered sugar. Soak in this six peeled almonds and, if possible, a crushed peach kernel, and allow to cool. When the mixture is cold add a dessertspoonful of Kirsch, one of Peach Brandy, a glass of Dry Vermouth and 2 glasses of any sweet white wine.
   Shake thoroughly with plenty of ice

American Beauty Cocktail

1 dash Crème de Menthe
¼ Orange Juice
¼ Grenadine
¼ Dry Vermouth
¼ Brandy
   Shake well and strain into medium-size glass and top with a little Port Wine

Americano Cocktail

⅓ Campari
⅔ Sweet Vermouth
lump of ice
   Use a wineglass. Fill with soda, stir, and add a twist of lemon peel

Cocktails

⅓ Dry Gin   *Angel Face Cocktail*
⅓ Apricot Brandy
⅓ Apple Brandy
   Shake well and strain into
   cocktail glass

½ Dry Gin   *Apparent Cocktail*
½ Dubonnet
1 dash Absinthe
   Stir well and strain into
   cocktail glass

½ Gin   *Appetizer Cocktail*
½ Dubonnet
juice of ½ orange
   Shake well and strain into
   cocktail glass

⅓ Sweet Cider   *Apple Cocktail*
⅙ Gin
⅙ Brandy
⅓ Apple Brandy
   Shake and serve

1 dash Angostura Bitters   *Applejack Cocktail*
½ Sweet Vermouth
½ Apple Brandy
   Shake well and strain into
   cocktail glass

Cocktails

Applejack Rabbit Cocktail
$\frac{1}{4}$ Apple Brandy
$\frac{1}{4}$ Lemon Juice
$\frac{1}{4}$ Orange Juice
$\frac{1}{4}$ Maple Syrup
Shake well and strain into cocktail glass

Applejack Special Cocktail
$\frac{2}{3}$ Apple Brandy
$\frac{1}{6}$ Grenadine
$\frac{1}{6}$ Lemon Juice
Shake well and strain into cocktail glass

Apple Pie Cocktail
$\frac{1}{2}$ Bacardi Rum
$\frac{1}{2}$ Sweet Vermouth
4 dashes Apricot Brandy
2 dashes Grenadine
4 dashes Lemon Juice
Shake well and strain into cocktail glass

Apricot Cocktail
$\frac{1}{4}$ Lemon Juice
$\frac{1}{4}$ Orange Juice
$\frac{1}{2}$ Apricot Brandy
1 dash Dry Gin
Shake well and strain into cocktail glass

Cocktails

Apricot Cocktail
(DRY)
(6 people)

Cut 2 apricots in half, break the stones and let the whole soak for 2 hours in a glass and a half of Cognac. Add 2 teaspoonfuls of Peach Bitters, 2 glasses of Gin and 2 glasses of Dry Vermouth
Shake well and strain into cocktail glasses

Apricot Cocktail
(SWEET)
(6 people)

Dilute a teaspoonful of Apricot Jam in a glass of Abricotine. Add a teaspoonful of Peach Bitters, slightly less than 2 glasses of Gin and $2\frac{1}{2}$ glasses of Dry Vermouth
Place this mixture in a shaker and put it on the ice to cool. When quite cold pour in two or three glasses of crushed ice and shake well. Strain into cocktail glasses

Artist's Special Cocktail

$\frac{1}{3}$ Whisky
$\frac{1}{3}$ Sherry
$\frac{1}{6}$ Lemon Juice
$\frac{1}{6}$ Groseille Syrup
Shake well and strain into cocktail glass

Cocktails

Astoria Cocktail

1 dash Orange Bitters
⅔ Gin
⅓ Dry Vermouth
Stir well and strain into cocktail glass. Serve with a stuffed olive

Atom Bomb Cocktail

½ Absinthe
½ Brandy
Stir and strain into cocktail glass

Atta Boy Cocktail

⅓ Dry Vermouth
⅔ Dry Gin
4 dashes Grenadine
Shake well and strain into cocktail glass

Atty Cocktail

¼ Dry Vermouth
3 dashes Absinthe
¾ Dry Gin
3 dashes Crème de Violette
Shake well and strain into cocktail glass

Aviation Cocktail

⅓ Lemon Juice
⅔ Dry Gin
2 dashes Maraschino
Shake well and strain into cocktail glass

Cocktails

¼ Dubonnet
¼ Dry Vermouth
¼ Sweet Vermouth
¼ Dry Gin
  Stir well with ice and strain
  into cocktail glass

Aviator Cocktail

¼ Lemon Juice or Lime Juice
¼ Grenadine
½ Bacardi Rum
  Shake well and strain into
  cocktail glass

Bacardi Cocktail

¼ Lemon Juice
¼ Cointreau
½ Vodka
  Shake and strain into
  cocktail glass. Serve with a
  twist of orange peel

Balalaika Cocktail

½ glass Orange Juice
½ glass Cointreau
3 glasses Sherry
1 dash Orange Bitters
2 dashes Pimento Dram
  Liqueur
  Fill up the shaker with
  cracked ice, shake and serve
  with an olive

Balm Cocktail
(6 people)

¼ Dry Vermouth
¼ Sweet Vermouth
½ Dry Sherry
  Stir well and strain into
  cocktail glass

Bamboo Cocktail

Cocktails

Banjino Cocktail

½ Gin
½ Orange Juice
dash of Crème de Banane
   Shake and strain into
   cocktail glass

Barney Barnato Cocktail

1 dash Angostura Bitters
1 dash Curaçao
½ Caperitif
½ Brandy
   Stir well and strain into
   cocktail glass

Baron Cocktail

6 dashes Curaçao
2 dashes Sweet Vermouth
⅓ Dry Vermouth
⅔ Dry Gin
   Shake well and strain into
   cocktail glass

Bartender Cocktail

¼ Gin
¼ Sherry
¼ Dubonnet
¼ Dry Vermouth
1 dash of Grand Marnier
   Stir and strain into cocktail
   glass

Cocktails

Beat up 4 eggs, and add
4 glasses Dry Gin
⅔ glass Cherry Brandy or
Curaçao
½ glass Lemon Juice
4 dashes Orange Bitters
½ tablespoonful powdered
sugar
1 tablespoonful Vanilla
flavouring
Shake well and strain into
medium-size glasses. Grate
nutmeg on top. Frost glasses
with castor sugar

Beautiful Cocktail

¼ Bacardi Rum
¼ Jamaica Rum
¼ Lemon Juice
⅛ Cointreau
⅛ Grenadine
Shake well and strain into
cocktail glass

Beaux Arts Cocktail

⅕ Amer Picon
⅕ Dry Vermouth
⅕ Sweet Vermouth
⅕ Forbidden Fruit
⅕ Dry Gin
Shake well with ice and
strain into cocktail glass

Cocktails

Belmont Cocktail

⅓ Grenadine
⅔ Dry Gin
1 teaspoonful fresh cream
Shake well and strain into
cocktail glass

Bennett Cocktail

2 dashes Angostura Bitters
¼ Lime Juice
¾ Dry Gin
Shake well and strain into
cocktail glass

Bentley Cocktail

½ Apple Brandy
½ Dubonnet
Shake well and strain into
cocktail glass

Berry Wall Cocktail

½ Dry Gin
½ Sweet Vermouth
4 dashes Curaçao
Shake well and strain into
cocktail glass. Squeeze
lemon peel on top

**Between-the-Sheets
Cocktail**

1 dash Lemon Juice
⅓ Brandy
⅓ Cointreau
⅓ Bacardi Rum
Shake well and strain into
cocktail glass

Cocktails

1 dash Angostura Bitters
⅓ Lillet
⅔ Dry Gin
Shake well and strain into
cocktail glass. Squeeze
orange peel on top

Bich's Special Cocktail

¼ Lemon Juice
¼ Swedish Punch
½ Dry Gin
Shake well and strain into
cocktail glass

Biffy Cocktail

½ Brandy
¼ Cointreau
¼ Sirop-de-Citron
Shake well and strain into
cocktail glass

Big Boy Cocktail

⅓ Gin
1 dash Orange Bitters
⅓ Green Chartreuse
⅓ Sweet Vermouth
Mix well with a spoon in a
large bar glass; strain into a
cocktail glass, add a cherry
or an olive, squeeze a piece of
lemon peel on top and serve

Bijou Cocktail

1 dash Orange Bitters
¼ Dubonnet
¼ Gin
½ Caperitif
Shake well and strain into
cocktail glass

Biltong Dry Cocktail

23

Cocktails

Bishop Cocktail

1 spirit measure Rum
1 teaspoonful Claret
1 dash Lemon Juice
a very little syrup
   Stir and strain into cocktail
   glass

Biter Cocktail

$\frac{1}{2}$ Gin
$\frac{1}{4}$ Lemon Juice, slightly
  sweetened
$\frac{1}{4}$ Green Chartreuse
1 dash of Absinthe
   Shake well and strain into
   cocktail glass

Black Velvet Cocktail

$\frac{1}{2}$ Stout
$\frac{1}{2}$ Champagne
   Use long tumbler. Pour very
   carefully

Blackthorn Cocktail

3 dashes Angostura Bitters
3 dashes Absinthe
$\frac{1}{2}$ Irish Whiskey
$\frac{1}{2}$ Dry Vermouth
   Shake well and strain into
   cocktail glass

Blanche Cocktail

$\frac{1}{3}$ Cointreau
$\frac{1}{3}$ Anisette
$\frac{1}{3}$ White Curaçao
   Shake well and strain into
   cocktail glass

Cocktails

1 dash Angostura Bitters
⅓ Dry Vermouth
⅔ Gin
  Stir well and strain into
  cocktail glass

Blenton Cocktail

½ Gin
¼ Dry Vermouth
⅛ Cherry Brandy
⅛ Peach Bitters
  Stir and strain into cocktail
  glass. Serve with a cherry

Blériot Cocktail

⅙ Absinthe
⅙ Apple Brandy
⅓ Brandy
⅓ Cointreau
  Shake and strain into
  cocktail glass

Block and Fall Cocktail

¼ Orange Juice
¼ Scotch Whisky
¼ Cherry Brandy
¼ Sweet Vermouth
  Shake well and strain into
  cocktail glass

Blood and Sand Cocktail

¼ Dry Vermouth
¼ Sweet Vermouth
½ Dry Gin
2 or 3 crushed Strawberries
  Use electric blender and
  strain into cocktail glass

Bloodhound Cocktail

25

Cocktails

Blood Transfusion Cocktail
½ Rum
½ juice of fresh Lime
Sweeten with Grenadine or
syrup. Shake and strain into
cocktail glass

Bloody Mary Cocktail
1½ oz. Vodka
2 oz. Tomato Juice
½ oz. Lemon Juice
2 dashes Worcestershire
Sauce
Shake and strain into
medium-size wineglass

Blue Bird Cocktail
4 dashes Angostura Bitters
1½ oz. Gin
5 dashes Orange Curaçao
Shake well and strain into
cocktail glass

Blue Blazer Cocktail

Use two large silver-plated mugs, with handles
1 wineglass Scotch Whisky
1 wineglass Boiling Water
Put the Whisky into one mug, and the boiling water into the
other, ignite the Whisky, and while blazing mix both
ingredients by pouring them four or five times from one
mug to the other. If done well this will look like a stream of
liquid fire
Sweeten with one teaspoonful of powdered white sugar,
and serve in a small bar tumbler, with a piece of
lemon peel

Cocktails

½ Dry Gin   *Blue Devil Cocktail*
¼ Lemon Juice or Lime Juice
¼ Maraschino
1 dash Blue Vegetable Extract
   Shake well and strain into
   cocktail glass

¼ Cointreau   *Blue Monday Cocktail*
¾ Vodka
1 dash Blue Vegetable Extract
   Shake well and strain into
   cocktail glass

Take 4 glasses of Whisky   *Blues Cocktail*
1 glass of Curaçao   *(6 people)*
Mix with 1 teaspoonful of
   Syrup of Prunes
   Pour out over plenty of
   cracked ice and shake for
   longer and more thoroughly
   than usual. Serve very cold

¼ Lemon Juice   *Blue Train Cocktail*
¼ Cointreau
½ Dry Gin
1 dash Blue Vegetable Extract
   Shake well and strain into
   cocktail glass

Cocktails

Blue Train Special Cocktail
(6 people)

Fill the shaker with cracked
ice and pour into it 2 oz. of
Brandy and 1 oz. of Pineapple
syrup. Shake carefully,
and then add 3 glasses of
Champagne. Give one or two
more shakes and serve at once

Bobby Burns Cocktail

½ Sweet Vermouth
½ Scotch Whisky
3 dashes Bénédictine
  Shake well and strain into
  cocktail glass. Squeeze
  lemon peel on top

Bolo Cocktail

juice of ¼ Lemon or ½ Lime
juice of ¼ Orange
1 oz. Bacardi Rum
1 teaspoonful sugar
  Shake well and strain into
  cocktail glass

Bombay Cocktail *(No. 1)*

¼ Lemon Juice
¾ East Indian Punch
  Shake well and strain into
  cocktail glass

Bombay Cocktail *(No. 2)*

1 dash Absinthe
2 dashes Curaçao
¼ Dry Vermouth
¼ Sweet Vermouth
½ Brandy
  Shake well and strain into
  cocktail glass

28

Cocktails

¼ Lemon Juice
¼ Drambuie
½ Scotch Whisky
   Shake and strain into
   cocktail glass

Bonnie Scot Cocktail

¼ Orange Juice
¼ Apple Brandy
½ Gin
a green cherry that has been
   macerated in orange
   Curaçao
   Shake well and strain into
   cocktail glass, afterwards
   adding the green cherry

*Booksellers' Special Pride
Cocktail*

1 dash Lemon Juice
1 dash Angostura Bitters
⅓ Dry Vermouth
⅓ Rye Whisky
⅓ Swedish Punch
   Shake well and strain into
   cocktail glass

Boomerang Cocktail

4 dashes Curaçao
white of 1 egg
2 oz. Brandy
   Shake well and strain into
   medium-size glass. Nutmeg
   on top

Booster Cocktail

Cocktails

Bosom Caresser Cocktail

yolk of 1 egg
1 teaspoon of Grenadine
⅓ Curaçao
⅔ Brandy
Shake well and strain into
medium-size glass

Brain-Storm Cocktail

2 oz. Irish Whiskey
2 dashes Bénédictine
2 dashes Dry Vermouth
Stir well and strain into
cocktail glass. Squeeze
orange peel on top

Cocktails

Brandy Cocktail

¼ Curaçao
¾ Brandy
   Stir well and strain into
   cocktail glass

Brandy Blazer Cocktail

Use a small thick glass
1 lump of sugar
1 piece of orange peel
1 piece of lemon peel
2 oz. Brandy
   Light with match, stir with
   long spoon for a few
   seconds and strain into
   cocktail glass

Brandy Crusta Cocktail

Use small wineglass. Moisten
the edge with lemon and dip
edge into castor sugar to
frost the glass
Cut the rind of half a lemon
spiral fashion; place in glass
Fill glass with cracked ice
3 dashes Maraschino
1 dash Angostura Bitters
4 dashes Lemon Juice
¼ Curaçao
¾ Brandy
   Stir well and strain into
   prepared glass, adding slice
   of orange

Cocktails

Brandy Gump Cocktail

½ Brandy
½ Lemon Juice
2 dashes Grenadine
Shake well and strain into cocktail glass

Brandy Vermouth Cocktail

1 dash Angostura Bitters
¼ Sweet Vermouth
¾ Brandy
Stir well and strain into cocktail glass

Brazil Cocktail

1 dash Angostura Bitters
1 dash Absinthe
½ Dry Vermouth
½ Sherry
Stir well and strain into cocktail glass. Squeeze lemon peel on top

Breakfast Cocktail

⅓ Grenadine
⅔ Dry Gin
white of 1 egg
Shake well and strain into large wineglass

Bridal Cocktail

⅓ Sweet Vermouth
⅔ Dry Gin
1 dash Orange Bitters
1 dash Maraschino
Orange peel on top
Shake well in ice and strain into cocktail glass

Cocktails

$\frac{1}{4}$ Lime Juice   *British Festival Cocktail*
$\frac{1}{4}$ Drambuie
$\frac{1}{2}$ Gin
Shake well in ice and strain
into cocktail glass

$\frac{1}{3}$ Crème de Cassis   *Broadway Smile Cocktail*
$\frac{1}{3}$ Swedish Punch
$\frac{1}{3}$ Cointreau
Use liqueur glass and pour
carefully so that ingredients
do not mix

$\frac{1}{2}$ Tequila   *Broadway Thirst Cocktail*
$\frac{1}{4}$ Orange Juice
$\frac{1}{4}$ Lemon Juice
1 teaspoonful Syrup
Shake well in ice and strain
into cocktail glass

yolk of 1 egg   *Broken Spur Cocktail*
$\frac{1}{6}$ Gin
$\frac{1}{6}$ Sweet Vermouth
$\frac{2}{3}$ White Port
1 teaspoonful Anisette
Shake well and strain into
cocktail glass

$\frac{1}{6}$ Orange Juice   *Bronx Cocktail*
$\frac{1}{6}$ Dry Vermouth
$\frac{1}{6}$ Sweet Vermouth
$\frac{1}{2}$ Dry Gin
Shake well and strain into
cocktail glass

Cocktails

Bronx Empress Cocktail

⅓ Dry Gin
⅓ Dry Vermouth
⅓ Orange Juice
few dashes Absinthe
    Shake well and strain into
    cocktail glass

Bronx Silver Cocktail

juice of ¼ Orange
white of 1 egg
¼ Dry Vermouth
¼ Sweet Vermouth
½ Dry Gin
    Shake well and strain into
    large wineglass

Bronx Terrace Cocktail

⅔ Gin
⅓ Dry Vermouth
juice of ½ Lime
    Shake well and strain into
    cocktail glass

Brooklyn Cocktail

1 dash Amer Picon
1 dash Maraschino
⅔ Rye Whisky
⅓ Dry Vermouth
    Shake well and strain into
    cocktail glass

Brunelle Cocktail

¼ Absinthe
½ tablespoonful sugar
¾ Lemon Juice
    Shake well and strain into
    cocktail glass

Cocktails

Put 2 or 3 lumps of ice into a
large tumbler, add the juice of
1 orange, 2 oz. of Gin, and fill
balance with Ginger Ale
  Stir and serve with a straw

Bull-Dog Cocktail

1½ oz. Vodka
2 oz. Cold Consommé
  Shake and strain into
  wine glass

Bull Shot Cocktail

2 dashes Angostura Bitters
½ Caperitif
½ Bacardi Rum
  Stir well and strain into
  cocktail glass

Bush-Ranger Cocktail

½ Pineapple Juice
½ Dry Gin
3 dashes Apricot Brandy
  Shake well and strain into
  cocktail glass

Butler Cocktail

⅓ Bacardi Rum
⅓ Dry Gin
⅓ Dry Vermouth
  Stir well and strain into
  cocktail glass

B.V.D. Cocktail

¼ Ginger
¼ Curaçao
¼ Port
¼ Sherry
  Shake and strain into
  cocktail glass

Byculla Cocktail

Cocktails

Byrrh Cocktail

$\frac{1}{3}$ Dry Vermouth
$\frac{1}{3}$ Rye Whisky
$\frac{1}{3}$ Byrrh
Stir well and strain into cocktail glass

Byrrh Cassis Cocktail

2 oz. Byrrh
1 oz. Crème de Cassis
Use medium-size glass and fill up with soda water

Cabaret Cocktail

1 dash Absinthe
1 dash Angostura Bitters
$\frac{1}{2}$ Dry Gin
$\frac{1}{2}$ Caperitif
Shake well and strain into cocktail glass. Add a cherry

Cablegram Cocktail

juice of $\frac{1}{2}$ Lemon
$\frac{1}{2}$ tablespoonful powdered sugar
2 oz. Rye Whisky
Shake well, strain into long tumbler and fill with ginger ale

Café de Paris Cocktail

white of 1 egg
3 dashes Anisette
1 teaspoonful fresh cream
2 oz. Dry Gin
Shake well and strain into medium-size glass

Cocktails

white of 1 egg
1 oz. Kirsch
½ tablespoonful sugar
2 oz. cold coffee
  Shake well and strain into
  medium-size glass

Café Kirsch Cocktail

4 oz. Apple Brandy
4 oz. Orange Juice
2 oz. Cointreau
2 oz. Orange Bitters
  Add plenty of ice and shake

Calvados Cocktail
(6 people)

⅓ Scotch Whisky
⅓ Irish Whiskey
⅙ Lemon Juice
⅙ Orgeat Syrup
  Shake well and strain into
  cocktail glass

Cameron's Kick Cocktail

½ Dry Gin
¼ Cointreau
¼ Lillet
  Shake well and strain into
  cocktail glass

Campden Cocktail

juice of ¼ Lemon
¼ tablespoonful powdered
  sugar
1 oz. Curaçao
3 dashes Rum
  Shake well and strain into
  cocktail glass

Canadian Cocktail

Cocktails

Canadian Whisky Cocktail
2 dashes Angostura Bitters
2 teaspoonfuls Gomme Syrup
2 oz. Rye Whisky
Shake well and strain into
cocktail glass

Cape Cocktail
⅓ Dry Gin
⅓ Caperitif
⅓ Orange Juice
Shake well and strain into
cocktail glass

Capetown Cocktail
1 dash Angostura Bitters
3 dashes Curaçao
½ Caperitif
½ Rye Whisky
Stir well and strain into
cocktail glass. Lemon peel
on top

Carrol Cocktail
⅔ Brandy
⅓ Sweet Vermouth
Stir well and strain into
cocktail glass. Add a pickled
walnut or onion

Caruso Cocktail
⅓ Dry Gin
⅓ Dry Vermouth
⅓ Green Crème de Menthe
Shake well and strain into
cocktail glass

38

Cocktails

2 dashes Maraschino
2 dashes Orange Bitters
2 dashes Lemon Juice
1 glass Gin
  Stir well and add a cherry

Casino Cocktail

½ Apple Brandy
½ White Crème de Menthe
3 dashes Absinthe
  Shake well and strain into
  cocktail glass

Castle Dip Cocktail

1 oz. fresh Lemon
1 oz. water
4 oz. Gin
½ oz. Kirsch
1 oz. Cointreau
3½ oz. Dry Vermouth
  Shake well and strain into
  cocktail glasses. Serve with
  an olive

Cat's-Eye Cocktail
(6 people)

⅙ Grenadine
⅙ Swedish Punch
⅙ Apple Brandy
⅙ Lemon Juice
⅓ Gin
  Shake well and strain into
  cocktail glass

C.F.H. Cocktail

Cocktails

Champagne Cocktail

Put into a champagne glass 1 lump of sugar and saturate it with Angostura Bitters. Fill the glass with cold Champagne and serve with a slice of orange. Add a teaspoonful of Brandy if desired

Champagne Cider or Perry Cocktail

Use Goblet. Small lump of ice. Add 4 drops of Angostura Bitters. Fill with Cider or Perry. Squeeze lemon peel on top. Add a slice of orange

Champs-Elysées Cocktail (6 people)

6 oz. Cognac
2 oz. Chartreuse
3 oz. sweetened Lemon Juice
1 dash Angostura Bitters
   Shake well and strain into cocktail glasses

Champagne Sidecar Cocktail

¼ Lemon Juice
½ Brandy
¼ Cointreau
   Shake and strain into a champagne glass. Fill up with Champagne

Chanticleer Cocktail

1 oz. Lemon Juice
1 oz. Raspberry Syrup
white of 1 egg
2 oz. Dry Gin
Shake well and strain into medium-size glass

Charleston Cocktail

$\frac{1}{6}$ Dry Gin
$\frac{1}{6}$ Kirsch
$\frac{1}{6}$ Maraschino
$\frac{1}{6}$ Curaçao
$\frac{1}{6}$ Dry Vermouth
$\frac{1}{6}$ Sweet Vermouth
Shake well and strain into cocktail glass. Squeeze lemon peel on top

Cherry Blossom Cocktail
(6 people)

1 oz. Curaçao
1 oz. Lemon Juice
1 oz. Grenadine
5 oz. Cherry Brandy
4 oz. Brandy
Shake thoroughly and serve very cold

Cherry Mixture Cocktail

1 dash Angostura Bitters
1 dash Maraschino
$\frac{1}{2}$ Dry Vermouth
$\frac{1}{2}$ Sweet Vermouth
Shake well and strain into cocktail glass. Serve with a cherry

Cocktails

Chicago Cocktail

1 dash Angostura Bitters
1 dash Curaçao
⅔ Brandy
Shake well and strain into cocktail glass. Frost edge of glass with castor sugar and fill with Champagne

Chinese Cocktail

1 dash Angostura Bitters
3 dashes Maraschino
3 dashes Curaçao
⅓ Grenadine
⅔ Rum
Shake well and strain into cocktail glass

Cocktails

1 teaspoonful powdered
chocolate
1 egg
1 oz. Maraschino
1 oz. Yellow Chartreuse
    Shake well and strain into
    large glass

Chocolate Cocktail (No. 1)

yolk of 1 fresh egg
¼ Yellow Chartreuse
¾ Port Wine
1 teaspoonful of Crushed
chocolate
    Shake well and strain into
    medium-size glass

Chocolate Cocktail (No. 2)

⅔ Whisky
⅓ Absinthe
1 dash Absinthe Bitters
    This cocktail is to be very
    thoroughly shaken and no
    sweetening in any form
    should be added

Choker Cocktail

3 dashes Absinthe
⅓ Bénédictine
⅔ Dry Vermouth
    Shake well and strain into
    cocktail glass. Squeeze
    orange peel on top

Chrysanthemum Cocktail

43

Cocktails

Church Parade Cocktail
$\frac{2}{3}$ Gin
1 dash Orange Curaçao
4 dashes Orange Juice
$\frac{1}{3}$ Dry Vermouth
Shake well and strain into
cocktail glass

Churchill Cocktail
$\frac{1}{2}$ Scotch Whisky
$\frac{1}{6}$ Lime Juice
$\frac{1}{6}$ Sweet Vermouth
$\frac{1}{6}$ Cointreau
Shake and strain into
cocktail glass

Claridge Cocktail
$\frac{1}{3}$ Dry Gin
$\frac{1}{3}$ Dry Vermouth
$\frac{1}{6}$ Apricot Brandy
$\frac{1}{6}$ Cointreau
Shake well and strain into
cocktail glass

Classic Cocktail
$\frac{1}{6}$ Lemon Juice
$\frac{1}{6}$ Curaçao
$\frac{1}{6}$ Maraschino
$\frac{1}{2}$ Brandy
Shake well and strain into
cocktail glass. Frost rim
of glass with castor sugar.
Squeeze lemon peel on top

Clover Club Cocktail
juice of $\frac{1}{2}$ Lemon or 1 Lime
white of 1 egg
$\frac{1}{3}$ Grenadine
$\frac{2}{3}$ Dry Gin
Shake well and strain into
medium-size glass

44

Cocktails

The same as *Clover Club* with
a sprig of fresh mint on top

Clover Leaf Cocktail

⅔ Dry Gin
⅓ Sweet Vermouth
1 dash Yellow Chartreuse
  Shake well and strain into
  cocktail glass

Club Cocktail

yolk of 1 egg
1 teaspoonful sugar or
  Gomme Syrup
⅓ Port Wine
⅙ Brandy
1 dash Curaçao
  Shake well, strain into a
  small wineglass, and grate a
  little nutmeg on top

Coffee Cocktail

This only *looks* like coffee—it has no coffee in its make-up

¼ White Crème de Menthe
¼ Sweet Vermouth
½ Brandy
  Shake well and strain into
  cocktail glass

Cold Deck Cocktail

⅔ Dry Gin
⅓ Grapefruit Juice
3 dashes Maraschino
  Shake well and strain into
  cocktail glass

Colonial Cocktail

Cocktails

Comet Cocktail
$\frac{3}{4}$ Gin
$\frac{1}{6}$ Strega
$\frac{1}{12}$ Van der Hum
Stir well with ice and serve
with a squeeze of lemon
rind

Commodore Cocktail
1 teaspoonful Syrup
2 dashes Orange Bitters
juice of $\frac{1}{2}$ Lime or $\frac{1}{4}$ Lemon
2 oz. Rye Whisky
Shake well and strain into
cocktail glass

Cooperstown Cocktail
$\frac{1}{3}$ Dry Vermouth
$\frac{1}{3}$ Sweet Vermouth
$\frac{1}{3}$ Dry Gin
Shake well and strain into
cocktail glass. Add a sprig
of mint

Cordova Cocktail
$\frac{2}{3}$ Dry Gin
1 dash Absinthe
1 teaspoonful fresh Cream
$\frac{1}{3}$ Sweet Vermouth
Shake well and strain into
cocktail glass

Coronation Cocktail
(No. 1)
$\frac{1}{2}$ Sherry
$\frac{1}{2}$ Dry Vermouth
1 dash Maraschino
2 dashes Orange Bitters
Shake well and strain into
cocktail glass

Cocktails

1 dash Peppermint
1 dash Peach Bitters
3 dashes Curaçao
⅔ Brandy
  Shake well and strain into
  cocktail glass

Coronation Cocktail
(No. 2)

⅔ Rye Whisky
⅓ cream
  cracked ice
  Shake well and strain into
  cocktail glass

Cowboy Cocktail

Cocktails

Creole Cocktail

$\frac{1}{2}$ Rye Whisky
$\frac{1}{2}$ Sweet Vermouth
2 dashes Bénédictine
2 dashes Amer Picon
Stir well and strain into cocktail glass. Twist lemon peel on top

Cresta Run Cocktail

$\frac{1}{2}$ Kirsch
$\frac{3}{8}$ Dry Vermouth
$\frac{1}{8}$ Crème de Noyaux
Stir and strain into cocktail glass. Add a twist of orange peel

Crow Cocktail

$\frac{1}{3}$ Rye Whisky
$\frac{2}{3}$ Lemon Juice
1 dash Grenadine
Shake well and strain into cocktail glass

Crystal Bronx Cocktail

juice of $\frac{1}{4}$ Orange
$\frac{1}{4}$ Dry Vermouth
$\frac{1}{4}$ Sweet Vermouth
lump of ice
Use medium-size glass and fill up with soda-water

Cuban Cocktail

juice of $\frac{1}{2}$ Lime or $\frac{1}{4}$ Lemon
$\frac{1}{3}$ Apricot Brandy
$\frac{2}{3}$ Brandy
Shake well and strain into cocktail glass

Cocktails

$\frac{1}{4}$ Lemon Juice
$\frac{1}{4}$ Lillet
$\frac{1}{4}$ Bacardi Rum
$\frac{1}{4}$ Apricot Brandy
   Shake well and strain into
   cocktail glass

Culross Cocktail

1 glass of Sherry
1 fresh egg
1 teaspoon powdered sugar
a little Cayenne Pepper
   Shake well and strain into
   medium-size glass

Cupid Cocktail

1 oz. Brandy
5 oz. Dark Curaçao
5 oz. Orange Juice
1 oz. Gin
   Shake and serve in glasses
   rinsed out with Orange Bitters

Curaçao Cocktail
(6 people)

1 teaspoonful powdered sugar
$\frac{1}{4}$ fresh Lime Juice
$\frac{3}{4}$ Bacardi Rum
   Shake well and strain into
   cocktail glass

Daiquiri Cocktail

$\frac{1}{2}$ fresh Lime Juice
1 teaspoonful powdered sugar
2 oz. Bacardi Rum
1 dash Maraschino
   Put into electric mixer with
   crushed ice, and pour
   unstrained into champagne
   glass. Add a cherry and
   serve with straws

Daiquiri (Frozen)
Cocktail

Cocktails

Damn-the-Weather Cocktail

3 dashes Curaçao
$\frac{1}{4}$ Orange Juice
$\frac{1}{4}$ Sweet Vermouth
$\frac{1}{2}$ Dry Gin
Shake well and strain into cocktail glass

D'Amour Cocktail

$\frac{1}{2}$ Gin
$\frac{1}{4}$ Anisette
$\frac{1}{4}$ fresh Lime Juice
white of 1 egg
Shake and strain into cocktail glass

Dandy Cocktail

$\frac{1}{2}$ Rye Whisky
$\frac{1}{2}$ Dubonnet
1 dash Angostura Bitters
3 dashes Cointreau
1 piece of Lemon Peel
1 piece of Orange Peel
Shake well and strain into cocktail glass

Darb Cocktail

$\frac{1}{3}$ Dry Vermouth
$\frac{1}{3}$ Dry Gin
$\frac{1}{3}$ Apricot Brandy
4 dashes Lemon Juice
Shake well and strain into cocktail glass

Davis Cocktail

$\frac{1}{4}$ Rum
$\frac{1}{2}$ Dry Vermouth
2 dashes Grenadine
juice of $\frac{1}{2}$ Lemon or 1 Lime
Shake well and strain into cocktail glass

Cocktails

1 dash Angostura Bitters
4 dashes Grenadine
⅓ Dry Vermouth
⅔ Brandy
  Shake well and strain into
  cocktail glass

Davis Brandy Cocktail

⅓ Champagne
⅓ Lime Juice
⅓ Sherry
  Shake and strain into
  cocktail glass

Dawn Cocktail

¼ Brandy
¼ Apple Brandy
¼ Cointreau
¼ Lemon Juice
  Shake well and strain into
  cocktail glass

Deauville Cocktail

⅓ Gin
⅓ Lemon Juice
⅙ Crème de Noyaux
⅙ Lime Juice
white of 1 egg
  Shake and strain into
  cocktail glass

Debutante Cocktail

1 dash Absinthe
1 dash Orange Bitters
½ Dry Vermouth
½ Gin
  Shake well and strain into
  cocktail glass. Add an olive
  and squeeze lemon peel on top

Deep Sea Cocktail

51

Cocktails

Dempsey Cocktail

2 dashes Absinthe
2 dashes Grenadine
½ Gin
½ Apple Brandy
Shake well and strain into
cocktail glass

Depth Bomb Cocktail

1 dash Lemon Juice
4 dashes Grenadine
½ Apple Brandy
½ Brandy
Shake well and strain into
cocktail glass

Depth-Charge Cocktail

2 dashes Absinthe
½ Lillet
½ Dry Gin
Shake well and strain into
cocktail glass. Squeeze
orange peel on top

*Depth-Charge Brandy
Cocktail*
(6 people)

5 oz. Brandy
5 oz. Apple Brandy
1 oz. Grenadine
2 oz. Lemon Juice
Shake and strain into
cocktail glass

Derby Cocktail

2 dashes Peach Bitters
2 sprigs fresh mint
2 oz. Dry Gin
Shake well and strain into
cocktail glass

Cocktails

½ Rye Whisky   *De Rigeur Cocktail*
¼ Grapefruit Juice
¼ honey
   Shake well and strain into
   cocktail glass

juice of 1 Orange   *Desert Healer Cocktail*
2 oz. Dry Gin
½ oz. Cherry Brandy
   Shake well, strain into long
   tumbler and fill with
   Ginger Beer

½ Port Wine   *Devil's Cocktail*
½ Dry Vermouth
2 dashes Lemon Juice
   Shake well and strain into
   cocktail glass

Pour into the shaker 8 oz. of   *Devonia Cocktail*
Sparkling Cider and 4 oz. of
Gin. Add some ice and a few
drops of Orange Bitters
   Shake lightly and serve

1 dash Lemon Juice   *Devonshire Pride Cocktail*
⅓ Swedish Punch
⅔ Apple Brandy
   Shake well and strain into
   cocktail glass

Cocktails

Diabola Cocktail

$\frac{2}{3}$ Dubonnet
$\frac{1}{3}$ Gin
2 dashes Orgeat Syrup
  Shake well and strain into
  cocktail glass

Diana Cocktail

Use Port wineglass
Fill with shaved ice
Fill glass $\frac{3}{4}$ full with White
Crème de Menthe and top
with Brandy

Diki-Diki Cocktail

$\frac{1}{6}$ Grapefruit Juice
$\frac{1}{6}$ Swedish Punch
$\frac{2}{3}$ Apple Brandy
  Shake well and strain into
  cocktail glass

Dinah Cocktail
(6 people)

First put 2 or 3 sprigs of
fresh mint in the shaker and
bruise them lightly against the
sides of the shaker by stirring
with a silver spoon. Pour into
the shaker 6 oz. of Rye
Whisky and let it stand for
some minutes. Add 6 oz. of
sweetened Lemon Juice and
some ice
  Shake very carefully and
  for longer than usual.
  Serve with a mint leaf
  standing in each glass

Cocktails

1 dash Maraschino
⅔ Dry Vermouth
⅓ Sweet Vermouth
  Shake well and strain into
  cocktail glass. Add a cherry
  and squeeze lemon peel on top

Diplomat Cocktail

½ Dry Gin
¼ Dry Vermouth
¼ Absinthe
  Shake well and strain into
  cocktail glass

Dixie Cocktail

To 2 lumps of sugar add a
small teaspoonful of
Angostura Bitters, another of
Lemon Juice, 8 oz. of
Bourbon Whisky, a small
teaspoonful of Curaçao and
2 teaspoonfuls of Crème de
Menthe
  Add plenty of ice, shake
  carefully and serve

Dixie Whisky Cocktail
(6 people)

⅓ Lemon Juice or Lime Juice
⅔ Swedish Punch
  Shake well and strain into
  cocktail glass

Doctor Cocktail

½ Gin
½ Cointreau
1 dash Grape Juice
  Shake well and strain into
  cocktail glass

Dodge Special Cocktail

Cocktails

Dolly O' Dare Cocktail

6 dashes Apricot Brandy
½ Dry Vermouth
½ Dry Gin
Shake well and strain into cocktail glass. Squeeze orange peel on top

Dream Cocktail

⅓ Curaçao
⅔ Brandy
1 dash Absinthe
Shake well and strain into cocktail glass

Du Barry Cocktail

1 dash Angostura Bitters
2 dashes Absinthe
⅓ Dry Vermouth
⅔ Gin
Shake well and strain into cocktail glass. Add slice of orange

Dubonnet Cocktail

½ Dubonnet
½ Dry Gin
Stir well and strain into cocktail glass

Duchess Cocktail

⅓ Dry Vermouth
⅓ Sweet Vermouth
⅓ Absinthe
Shake well and strain into cocktail glass

Cocktails

½ Sherry
½ Sweet Vermouth
3 dashes Orange Bitters
  Stir well and twist orange
  peel on top

*Duke of Marlborough
Cocktail*

In a shaker with cracked ice
place a teaspoonful of
Curaçao, 4 oz. of Gin, 4 oz. of
Sherry and 4 oz. of Dry
Vermouth
  Stir thoroughly with a
  spoon, shake, strain and
  serve. Add an olive and
  2 dashes of Absinthe
  to each glass

Dunhill's Special Cocktail
(6 people)

1 dash Angostura Bitters
⅓ Sherry
⅔ Rum
  Stir well and strain into
  cocktail glass

Dunlop Cocktail

Pour 9 oz. of Whisky into a
large glass and soak in this a
few cloves. Add 5 or 6 drops
of Orange Bitters and lastly
put in 3 oz. of Curaçao
  Put it all in the shaker;
  shake and serve

Duppy Cocktail
(6 people)

Cocktails

Eagle's Dream Cocktail

1 teaspoonful powdered
  sugar
white of 1 egg
juice of $\frac{1}{4}$ Lemon
$\frac{1}{4}$ Crème Yvette
$\frac{3}{4}$ Dry Gin
Shake well and strain into
medium-size glass

East India Cocktail

$\frac{1}{8}$ Pineapple Juice
$\frac{1}{8}$ Orange Curaçao
1 dash Angostura Bitters
$\frac{3}{4}$ Brandy
Stir well and strain into
cocktail glass

Eclipse Cocktail

$\frac{1}{3}$ Dry Gin
$\frac{2}{3}$ Sloe Gin
Put enough Grenadine in a
cocktail glass to cover a
ripe olive. Mix the spirits
together and pour gently
on to the Grenadine so that
it does not mix. Squeeze
orange peel on top

Eddie Brown Cocktail

2 dashes Apricot Brandy
$\frac{1}{3}$ Lillet
$\frac{2}{3}$ Dry Gin
Shake well and strain into
cocktail glass. Squeeze
lemon peel on top

Cocktails

½ Prunelle Brandy
2 dashes Dry Vermouth
½ Dry Gin
   Shake well and strain into
   cocktail glass

Elk Cocktail

white of 1 egg
½ Rye Whisky
½ Port Wine
juice of ½ Lemon
1 teaspoon sugar
   Shake well, strain into
   wineglass and add a slice of
   pineapple

Elk's Own Cocktail

¼ Apricot Brandy
¼ Apple Brandy
½ Gin
   Shake well and strain into
   cocktail glass

Empire Cocktail

juice of ½ Lemon
½ tablespoonful powdered
   sugar
¼ Kirsch
¾ Gin
   Shake well and strain into
   long tumbler. Fill up with
   soda-water

Eton Blazer Cocktail

3 dashes Green Mint
6 dashes Green Chartreuse
2 oz. Irish Whiskey
   Shake and strain into cocktail
   glass. Add a green olive

*"Everybody's Irish"
Cocktail*

Cocktails

Eve's Apple Cocktail

⅓ Applejack
⅓ Swedish Punch
⅓ Grapefruit Juice
Shake well and strain into cocktail glass

Fair and Warmer Cocktail

⅓ Sweet Vermouth
⅔ Bacardi Rum
2 dashes Curaçao
Shake well and strain into cocktail glass

Fairbanks Cocktail (No. 1)

1 dash Lemon Juice
1 dash Grenadine
⅓ Apricot Brandy
⅓ Dry Vermouth
⅓ Dry Gin
Shake well and strain into cocktail glass with a cherry

Fairbanks Cocktail (No. 2)

2 dashes Crème de Noyau
2 dashes Orange Bitters
⅓ Dry Vermouth
⅔ Dry Gin
Shake well and strain into cocktail glass

Fairy Belle Cocktail

white of 1 egg
1 teaspoonful Grenadine
¼ Apricot Brandy
¾ Dry Gin
Shake well and strain into Port wineglass

Cocktails

1 dash Angostura Bitters
2 dashes Crème de Menthe
juice of 1 Lemon or ½ Lime
2 oz. Dry Gin
  Shake well and strain into
  cocktail glass

Fallen Angel Cocktail

Pour into the shaker 10 oz. of
Cognac and ½ oz. of
Angostura Bitters. Shake
thoroughly and serve, adding
a little Champagne and a
piece of lemon peel after
having rubbed the edges of
the glasses with Lemon
Syrup

Fancy Cocktail
(6 people)

2 dashes Absinthe
⅓ Dry Vermouth
⅔ Dry Gin
1 sprig fresh mint
  Shake well and strain into
  cocktail glass

Fascinator Cocktail

1 dash Lemon Juice
⅓ Apricot Brandy
⅓ Dry Vermouth
⅓ Dry Gin
  Shake well and strain into
  cocktail glass

Favourite Cocktail

Cocktails

Fine and Dandy Cocktail
¼ Lemon Juice
¼ Cointreau
½ Gin
1 dash Angostura Bitters
Shake well and strain into
cocktail glass

Five-Fifteen Cocktail
⅓ Curaçao
⅓ Dry Vermouth
⅓ sweet cream
Shake well and strain into
cocktail glass

'Flu Cocktail
juice of ¼ Lemon
1 dash Ginger
¼ oz. Rock Candy Syrup
¼ oz. Ginger Brandy
2 oz. Rye Whisky
Stir well and strain into
medium-size glass, but do
not ice

Fluffy Ruffles Cocktail
½ Bacardi Rum
½ Sweet Vermouth
peel of 1 Lime or piece of
Lemon
Shake well and strain into
cocktail glass

Flying Scotchman Cocktail
(6 people)
5 oz. Sweet Vermouth
6 oz. Scotch Whisky
1 oz. Bitters
1 oz. Sugar Syrup
Shake well and strain into
cocktail glasses

Cocktails

1 dash Grenadine or Syrup
¼ Dry Vermouth
¼ Swedish Punch
½ Bacardi Rum
  Shake well and strain into
  cocktail glass

Four Flush Cocktail

⅓ Dry Vermouth
⅓ Gin
⅓ Sweet Vermouth
4 dashes Absinthe
  Shake well and strain into
  cocktail glass

Fourth Degree Cocktail

½ Brandy
⅓ Lillet
⅙ Yellow Chartreuse
  Stir and strain into cocktail
  glass. Add a twist of lemon
  peel

Four Score Cocktail

4 dashes Peach Bitters
1 lump of ice
¼ Crème de Cacao
¾ Rye Whisky
  Use wineglass and squeeze
  lemon peel on top

Fox River Cocktail

juice of ½ Lemon or 1 Lime
2 dashes Orange Curaçao
2 oz. Bacardi Rum
  Shake well and strain into
  cocktail glass

Fox Trot Cocktail

63

Cocktails

Frankenjack Cocktail

⅓ Gin
⅓ Dry Vermouth
⅙ Apricot Brandy
⅙ Cointreau
　Shake well and strain into
　cocktail glass

Frank Sullivan Cocktail

¼ Lemon Juice
¼ Lillet
¼ Cointreau
¼ Brandy
　Shake well and strain into
　cocktail glass

French "75" Cocktail

⅔ Gin
⅓ Lemon Juice
1 spoonful powdered sugar
　Pour into tall glass
　containing cracked ice and
　fill up with Champagne

Froth Blower Cocktail

white of 1 egg
¼ oz. Grenadine
2 oz. Gin
　Shake well and strain into
　Port wineglass

Froupe Cocktail

3 dashes Bénédictine
½ Sweet Vermouth
½ Brandy
　Stir well and strain into
　cocktail glass

Cocktails

¼ Swedish Punch
¼ Dry Vermouth
½ Bacardi Rum
  Shake well and strain into
  cocktail glass

Full House Cocktail

6 oz. Gin
6 oz. Absinthe
  Add, if required, a very
  little sugar. Shake well and
  serve

Gasper Cocktail
(6 people)

3 dashes Syrup
3 dashes Lemon Juice
½ Sweet Vermouth
½ Brandy
  Shake well and strain into
  cocktail glass

Gazette Cocktail

1 dash Orange Juice
1 dash Lemon Juice
⅓ Dry Vermouth
⅔ Gin
  Shake well and strain into
  cocktail glass

Gene Tunney Cocktail

⅐ Dry Vermouth
6/7 Gin
  Shake well and strain into
  cocktail glass. Squeeze
  lemon peel on top and add
  an onion

Gibson Cocktail

Cocktails

Gilroy Cocktail

$\frac{1}{6}$ Lemon Juice
$\frac{1}{6}$ Dry Vermouth
$\frac{1}{3}$ Cherry Brandy
$\frac{1}{3}$ Dry Gin
1 dash Orange Bitters
Shake well and strain into cocktail glass

Gimlet Cocktail

$\frac{1}{2}$ Gin
$\frac{1}{2}$ Lime Juice Cordial
Use Old-Fashioned glass, stir, add ice, and serve

Gin Cocktail

4 dashes Orange Bitters
2 oz. Dry Gin
Shake well and strain into cocktail glass

Gin and Cape Cocktail

$\frac{1}{2}$ Caperitif
$\frac{1}{2}$ Dry Gin
Stir well and strain into cocktail glass

Glad Eye Cocktail

$\frac{1}{3}$ Peppermint
$\frac{2}{3}$ Absinthe
Shake well and strain into cocktail glass

Glider Cocktail

$\frac{3}{4}$ Dry Gin
1 dash Absinthe
2 dashes Grenadine
$\frac{1}{4}$ Lime Juice
white of 1 egg
Shake well and strain into cocktail glass

Cocktails

¼ Lemon Juice   *Gloom Chaser Cocktail*
¼ Grenadine
¼ Grand Marnier
¼ Curaçao
  Shake well and strain into
  cocktail glass

1 dash Grenadine   *Golden Dawn Cocktail*
¼ Orange Juice
¼ Apricot Brandy
¼ Apple Brandy
¼ Dry Gin
  Put Grenadine in glass first
  and pour Cocktail very
  carefully over Grenadine

¾ Orange Ice   *Golden Gate Cocktail*
¼ Gin
  Place in shaker and shake.
  No ice

½ oz. Yellow Chartreuse   *Golden Slipper Cocktail*
yolk of 1 fresh egg
½ oz. Eau de Vie de Danzig
  Shake well and strain into
  cocktail glass

⅙ Apricot Brandy   *Good Night Ladies*
⅙ Grenadine   *Cocktail*
½ Dry Gin
⅙ Lemon Juice
  Shake well and strain into
  cocktail glass

Cocktails

Grace's Delight Cocktail
(6 people)

Fill a large glass with broken ice and place in it 4 oz. of Whisky, 5 oz. of Dry Vermouth and 1 oz. of Raspberry Brandy. Add the juice of half an orange, a teaspoonful of Orange-flower water, 3 juniper berries, and a little cinnamon and nutmeg
Stir well with a bar spoon and pour the mixture, straining it, into a cocktail-shaker holding about a pint. Shake and keep for an hour on ice, then serve

Gradeal Special Cocktail

¼ Dry Gin
¼ Apricot Brandy
½ Bacardi Rum
Shake well and strain into cocktail glass

Grand Royal Clover Club Cocktail

juice of ½ Lemon
1 oz. Grenadine
1 egg
2 oz. Dry Gin
Shake well and strain into medium-size glass

Grand Slam Cocktail

¼ Dry Vermouth
¼ Sweet Vermouth
½ Swedish Punch
Shake well and strain into cocktail glass

68

Cocktails

¼ Grape Juice
¼ Lemon Juice
½ Gin
1 dash Grenadine
   Shake well and strain into
   cocktail glass

Grape Vine Cocktail

juice of 1½ Lemons
2 teaspoonfuls Grapefruit
   Jelly
8 oz. Gin
   Add ice and shake. (Any
   other fruit jelly of
   distinctive taste may be
   used)

Grapefruit Cocktail
(6 people)

1 dash Angostura Bitters
⅓ Lillet
⅔ Dry Gin
   Shake well and strain into
   cocktail glass. Squeeze
   orange peel on top

Great Secret Cocktail

1 dash Peach Bitters
⅓ Dry Vermouth
⅔ Sherry
1 sprig fresh mint
   Shake well and strain into
   cocktail glass

Greenbriar Cocktail

Cocktails

Green Dragon Cocktail

⅛ Lemon Juice
⅛ Kummel
¼ Green Mint
½ Dry Gin
4 dashes Peach Bitters
Shake well and strain into
cocktail glass

Green-eyed Monster Cocktail

⅓ Dry Gin
⅓ Sweet Vermouth
⅓ Green Chartreuse
Stir with ice and strain into
cocktail glass

Green Room Cocktail

⅓ Brandy
⅔ Dry Vermouth
2 dashes Curaçao
Shake well and strain into
cocktail glass

Cocktails

1 dash Ginger
⅓ Ginger Brandy
⅔ Brandy
1 teaspoonful powdered sugar
Shake well and strain into
cocktail glass

Grenadier Cocktail

2 dashes Curaçao
⅓ Sweet Vermouth
⅔ Dry Gin
Shake well and strain into
cocktail glass

Guard's Cocktail

2 dashes Curaçao
⅓ Lillet
⅔ Dry Gin
Shake well and strain into
cocktail glass. Squeeze
orange peel on top

H. and H. Cocktail

⅔ Rye Whisky
⅙ Dry Vermouth
⅙ Maple Syrup
1 dash Angostura Bitters

Habitant Cocktail

1 dash Orange Bitters
2 dashes Curaçao
½ Dry Gin
½ Sweet Vermouth
Shake well and strain into
cocktail glass

Hakam Cocktail

Cocktails

Hanky Panky Cocktail

2 dashes Fernet Branca
½ Sweet Vermouth
½ Dry Gin
Shake well and strain into
cocktail glass. Squeeze
orange peel on top

Happy Return Cocktail

½ Gin
¼ Cointreau
⅙ Cherry Brandy
$\frac{1}{12}$ fresh Lemon Juice
Shake and strain into
cocktail glass. Serve with a
cherry on a pink stick

Harrovian Cocktail

1 dash Angostura Bitters
¼ oz. Orange Juice
1 dash Lemon Juice
2 oz. Dry Gin
Shake well and strain into
cocktail glass

Harry Lauder Cocktail

½ Scotch Whisky
½ Sweet Vermouth
2 dashes Grenadine
Stir and strain into cocktail
glass

Harry's Cocktail

⅓ Sweet Vermouth
1 dash Absinthe
⅔ Gin
2 sprigs fresh mint
Shake well and strain into
cocktail glass. Serve with
a stuffed olive

72

Cocktails

2 dashes Angostura Bitters
1 dash Syrup
½ Brandy
½ Sweet Vermouth
   Shake well and strain into
   cocktail glass

Harvard Cocktail

1 dash Absinthe
4 dashes Grenadine
⅓ Dry Vermouth
⅔ Gin
   Shake well and strain into
   cocktail glass

Hasty Cocktail

1 dash Lemon Juice
¼ Dry Gin
¼ Swedish Punch
½ Apricot Brandy
   Shake well and strain into
   cocktail glass

Havana Cocktail

½ Gin
¼ Orange Juice
¼ Curaçao (or any other of
   the Orange Liqueurs)
   Shake well and strain into
   cocktail glass

Hawaiian Cocktail

Shake 6 oz. of Cognac and
6 oz. of Green Crème de
Menthe. Serve with a pinch of
red pepper on each glass

Hell Cocktail
(6 people)

Cocktails

Hesitation Cocktail

1 dash Lemon Juice
¼ Rye Whisky
¾ Swedish Punch
Shake well and strain into
cocktail glass

Hibiscus Cocktail

juice of ½ Lime
1 dash Grenadine
2 oz. Rum
Shake and strain into
cocktail glass

High Flyer Cocktail

¼ Strega
$\frac{1}{12}$ Van der Hum
⅔ Gin
Stir and strain into cocktail
glass. Serve with a squeeze
of lemon peel

Hildebrande Cocktail

1 lump of sugar
2 dashes Angostura Bitters
2 oz. Scotch Whisky
Crush sugar and Bitters
together. Add lump of ice,
twist of lemon peel, slice of
orange, sprig of fresh mint.
Use a small stem glass and
serve with a spoon

Holland House Cocktail

juice of ¼ Lemon
1 slice of Pineapple
⅓ Dry Vermouth
⅔ Dry Gin
4 dashes Maraschino
Shake well and strain into
cocktail glass

Cocktails

1 slice of Orange   *Homestead Cocktail*
⅔ Dry Gin
⅓ Sweet Vermouth
   Shake well and strain into
   cocktail glass

juice of ½ Lemon   *Honeymoon Cocktail*
3 dashes Curaçao
½ Bénédictine
½ Apple Brandy
   Shake well and strain into
   cocktail glass

1 dash Angostura Bitters   *Honolulu Cocktail (No. 1)*
1 dash Orange Juice
1 dash Pineapple Juice
1 dash Lemon Juice
2 oz. Dry Gin
a little powdered sugar
   Shake well and strain into
   cocktail glass

⅓ Maraschino   *Honolulu Cocktail (No. 2)*
⅓ Gin
⅓ Bénédictine
   Shake well and strain into
   cocktail glass

¼ Lemon Juice   *"Hoopla!" Cocktail*
¼ Lillet
¼ Cointreau
¼ Brandy
   Shake well and strain into
   cocktail glass

Cocktails

"Hoots Mon" Cocktail
$\frac{1}{4}$ Lillet
$\frac{1}{4}$ Sweet Vermouth
$\frac{1}{2}$ Scotch Whisky
Stir well and strain into
cocktail glass

Hop Toad Cocktail
$\frac{1}{4}$ Lemon Juice
$\frac{3}{4}$ Apricot Brandy
Shake well and strain into
cocktail glass

Hotcha Cocktail
$\frac{2}{3}$ Rum
$\frac{1}{3}$ Sherry
Stir in ice and strain into
cocktail glass

Hot Deck Cocktail
1 dash Ginger
$\frac{1}{4}$ Sweet Vermouth
$\frac{3}{4}$ Rye Whisky
Shake well and strain into
cocktail glass

Houla-Houla Cocktail
1 dash Curaçao
$\frac{1}{3}$ Orange Juice
$\frac{2}{3}$ Dry Gin
Shake well and strain into
cocktail glass

Hundred per Cent Cocktail
$\frac{1}{6}$ Orange Juice
$\frac{1}{6}$ Lemon Juice
$\frac{2}{3}$ Swedish Punch
2 dashes Grenadine
Shake well and strain into
cocktail glass

Cocktails

yolk of 1 egg
1 Port wineglass milk
¼ Orange Curaçao
¾ Brandy
  Shake well and strain into
  medium-size glass, with
  nutmeg on top

Ichbien Cocktail

3 dashes Maraschino
⅓ Dry Vermouth
⅔ Dry Gin
1 tablespoonful Grapefruit
  Juice
  Shake well and strain into
  cocktail glass. Serve small
  nut in glass

Ideal Cocktail

1 dash Maraschino
1 dash Angostura Bitters
½ Dry Vermouth
½ Dry Gin
  Stir well and serve with an
  olive

Imperial Cocktail

1 dash Orgeat Syrup
1 dash Orange Bitters
¼ Gin
¼ Sherry
¼ Dry Vermouth
¼ Sweet Vermouth
  Shake well and strain into
  cocktail glass

Inca Cocktail

Cocktails

Income Tax Cocktail

1 dash Angostura Bitters
juice of $\frac{1}{4}$ Orange
$\frac{1}{4}$ Dry Vermouth
$\frac{1}{4}$ Sweet Vermouth
$\frac{1}{2}$ Dry Gin
Shake well and strain into
cocktail glass

Ink Street Cocktail

$\frac{1}{3}$ Rye Whisky
$\frac{1}{3}$ Orange Juice
$\frac{1}{3}$ Lemon Juice
Shake well and strain into
cocktail glass

Iolanthe Cocktail

$\frac{1}{3}$ Brandy
$\frac{1}{3}$ Lillet
$\frac{1}{6}$ Grand Marnier
$\frac{1}{6}$ Orange Juice
3 dashes Orange Bitters
Shake and strain into
cocktail glass

Irish Cocktail

2 dashes Absinthe
2 dashes Curaçao
1 dash Maraschino
1 dash Angostura Bitters
1 oz. Irish Whiskey
Shake well and strain into
cocktail glass, add olive and
squeeze orange peel on top

Cocktails

2 dashes Orange Bitters
⅓ Dry Gin
⅓ Dry Sherry
⅓ Caperitif
Stir well and strain into
cocktail glass. Squeeze
lemon peel on top

Jabberwock Cocktail

¼ Bacardi Rum
1 dash Lemon Juice
1 dash syrup
¾ Dry Gin
Shake well and strain into
cocktail glass

Jack Kearns Cocktail

¼ Orange Juice
1 slice of Pineapple
½ Dry Gin
¼ Dry Vermouth
Shake well and strain into
cocktail glass

Jack Pine Cocktail

¼ Lemon or Lime Juice
¼ Grenadine
½ Applejack
Shake well and strain into
cocktail glass

Jack Rose Cocktail

2 dashes Orange Bitters
½ Orange Gin
½ Dubonnet
Stir well and strain into
cocktail glass

Jackson Cocktail

Cocktails

Jersey Lightning Cocktail

1 dash Angostura Bitters
¼ Sweet Vermouth
¼ Apple Brandy
½ Brandy
Shake well and strain into
cocktail glass

Jewel Cocktail
(6 people)

4 oz. Green Chartreuse
4 oz. Sweet Vermouth
4 oz. Gin
¼ oz. Orange Bitters
Shake thoroughly and
serve with a cherry,
squeezing lemon peel on top

Jeyplak Cocktail

1 dash Absinthe
⅔ Dry Gin
⅓ Sweet Vermouth
Shake well and strain into
cocktail glass. Squeeze
lemon peel on top

Jimmy Blanc Cocktail

3 dashes Dubonnet
⅓ Lillet
⅔ Dry Gin
Shake well and strain into
cocktail glass. Squeeze
orange peel on top

Joburg Cocktail

4 dashes Orange Bitters
½ Caperitif
½ Bacardi Rum
Stir well and strain into
cocktail glass. Squeeze
lemon peel on top

Cocktails

1 dash Orange Bitters
1 dash Angostura Bitters
2 dashes Crème de Noyau
4 dashes Lemon Juice
¾ glass Dry Gin
  Shake well and strain into
  cocktail glass

Jockey Club Cocktail

3 dashes Absinthe
⅓ Orange Curaçao
⅔ Sloe Gin
  Shake well and strain into
  cocktail glass

Johnnie Mack Cocktail

²⁄₉ Irish Whiskey
⁴⁄₉ Sweet Vermouth
²⁄₉ Lemon Juice]
⅑ Kummel
1 dash Angostura Bitters
  Shake well and strain into
  cocktail glass

John Wood Cocktail

1 dash Orange Bitters
1 dash Lemon Juice or
  Lime Juice
1 dash Brandy
⅓ Sweet Vermouth
⅓ Dry Vermouth
⅓ Dry Gin
  Shake well and strain into
  cocktail glass. Squeeze
  lemon peel on top

J.O.S. Cocktail

81

Cocktails

Journalist Cocktail

2 dashes Lemon Juice
2 dashes Curaçao
1 dash Angostura Bitters
$\frac{1}{6}$ Dry Vermouth
$\frac{1}{6}$ Sweet Vermouth
$\frac{2}{3}$ Dry Gin
Shake well in ice and strain into cocktail glass

Judgette Cocktail

$\frac{1}{3}$ Peach Brandy
$\frac{1}{3}$ Gin
$\frac{1}{3}$ Dry Vermouth
1 dash Lime
Shake well and strain into cocktail glass

Jupiter Cocktail

1 teaspoonful Orange Juice
1 teaspoonful Parfait Amour Liqueur
$\frac{1}{3}$ Dry Vermouth
$\frac{2}{3}$ Dry Gin
Shake well and strain into cocktail glass

Karl K. Kitchen Cocktail

$\frac{1}{4}$ white Grape Juice
4 dashes Grenadine or Syrup
$\frac{3}{4}$ Scotch Whisky
Shake well and strain into cocktail glass

K.C.B. Cocktail

1 dash Apricot Brandy
1 dash Lemon Juice
$\frac{1}{4}$ Kirsch
$\frac{3}{4}$ Dry Gin
Shake well and strain into cocktail glass

Cocktails

2 dashes Sweet Vermouth
⅓ Apple Brandy
⅔ Bacardi Rum
  Shake well and strain into
  cocktail glass

Kicker Cocktail

¼ Lillet
½ Dry Gin
¼ Sweet Vermouth
  Shake well and strain into
  cocktail glass

Kina Cocktail

Cocktails

King Cole Cocktail

1 glass Rye Whisky
2 dashes Syrup
1 dash Fernet Branca
1 lump of ice
Stir well and decorate with
slices of orange and
pineapple

Kingston Cocktail

½ Rum
¼ Kummel
¼ Orange Juice
1 dash Pimento Dram
Shake carefully and serve
while it is frothing

Knicker-Bocker Special Cocktail

1 teaspoonful Raspberry
Syrup
1 teaspoonful Lemon Juice
1 teaspoonful Orange Juice
⅔ Rum
2 dashes Curaçao
Shake well and strain into
cocktail glass. Add chunk of
pineapple

Knock-out Cocktail

1 teaspoonful White Crème
de Menthe
⅓ Absinthe
⅓ Dry Gin
⅓ Dry Vermouth
Shake well and strain into
cocktail glass

Cocktails

1 dash Absinthe
⅛ Sweet Vermouth
¼ Dry Vermouth
⅝ Dry Gin
  Shake well and strain into
  cocktail glass. Squeeze
  orange peel on top

Kup's Indispensable
Cocktail

2 dashes Absinthe
2 dashes Anisette
2 dashes Angostura Bitters
2 oz. Rye Whisky
  Stir well and put small piece
  of pineapple in glass

Ladies Cocktail

⅓ Grape Juice
⅓ Swedish Punch
⅓ Dry Gin
  Shake well and strain into
  cocktail glass

Lasky Cocktail

1 dash Absinthe
1 dash Maraschino
1 dash Angostura Bitters
⅓ Dry Vermouth
⅔ Rye Whisky
  Shake well and strain into
  cocktail glass

Lawhill Cocktail

½ Gin
¼ Dry or Sweet Vermouth
¼ Curaçao
white of 1 egg
  Shake well with ice and
  strain into cocktail glass

League of Nations
Cocktail

Cocktails

Leap-frog Cocktail

1 lump of ice
juice of ½ Lemon
2 oz. Gin
1 split of Ginger Ale
Serve in a long tumbler

Leap Year Cocktail

1 dash Lemon Juice
⅔ Gin
⅙ Grand Marnier
⅙ Sweet Vermouth
Shake well and serve in
cocktail glass. Squeeze
lemon peel on top

Leave It to Me Cocktail

1 dash Lemon Juice
¼ Apricot Brandy
¼ Dry Vermouth
1 dash Grenadine
½ Gin
Shake well and strain into
cocktail glass

Le Chantecleer Cocktail

⅓ Gin
⅓ Lemon Juice
⅙ Bénédictine
⅙ Crème de Noyau (white)
Shake well and strain into
cocktail glass

Lemon Pie Cocktail

2 oz. Scotch Whisky
1 bottle Lemonade

Cocktails

1 dash Syrup
⅓ Bacardi Rum
⅔ Applejack
   Shake well and strain into
   cocktail glass

Liberty Cocktail

1 dash Lemon Juice
⅓ Dry Gin
⅓ Lillet
⅓ Crème de Noyau
   Shake well and strain into
   cocktail glass

Lily Cocktail

⅓ Brandy
⅓ Lillet
⅓ Lemon Juice
1 dash White Curaçao
   Shake well and strain into
   cocktail glass

Lilliput Cocktail

½ Whisky
½ sweetened Pineapple Juice
1 dash Absinthe Bitters
   Shake and serve, squeezing
   a little lemon peel on top

Linstead Cocktail

⅙ Lemon Juice
⅙ Cointreau
⅓ Bacardi Rum
⅓ Dry Gin
   Shake well and strain into
   cocktail glass

Little Devil Cocktail

Cocktails

Little Princess Cocktail

½ Sweet Vermouth
½ Bacardi Rum
  Shake well and strain into
  cocktail glass

Londino Cocktail

¼ Gin
¼ Orange Juice
¼ Dry Vermouth
⅛ Campari
⅛ Apricot Brandy
  Shake well and strain into
  cocktail glass

London Cocktail

2 dashes Orange Bitters
2 dashes Syrup
2 dashes Absinthe
  Dry Gin
  Shake well and strain into
  cocktail glass

Lone Tree Cocktail

2 dashes Orange Bitters
⅓ Sweet Vermouth
⅓ Dry Vermouth
⅓ Dry Gin
  Shake well and strain into
  cocktail glass

Lord Suffolk Cocktail

⅛ Sweet Vermouth
⅛ Cointreau
⅝ Dry Gin
⅛ Maraschino
  Shake well and strain into
  cocktail glass

Cocktails

½ Gin
¼ Lillet
¼ Grand Marnier
  Stir well and strain into
  cocktail glass

Lorraine Cocktail

Juice of 1 Lemon
8 oz. Rye Whisky
4 teaspoonfuls sugar
1 egg
1 dash Sweet Vermouth
  Shake well and strain into
  cocktail glasses

Los Angeles Cocktail
(4 people)

1 teaspoonful Grenadine
1 dash Cointreau
juice of ½ Tangerine
½ Dry Gin
½ Dry Vermouth
  Shake well and strain into
  cocktail glass

Luigi Cocktail

¼ Lemon Juice
¼ Orange Juice
½ Cointreau
  Shake well and strain into
  cocktail glass

Lulu's Favourite Cocktail

⅔ Dry Vermouth
⅓ Brandy
1 dash Orange Bitters
1 dash Absinthe
  Stir and strain into
  cocktail glass

Lusitania Cocktail

Cocktails

Lutkins Special Cocktail
2 dashes Orange Juice
2 dashes Apricot Brandy
$\frac{1}{2}$ Dry Vermouth
$\frac{1}{2}$ Dry Gin
Shake well and strain into cocktail glass

Macaroni Cocktail
$\frac{1}{3}$ Sweet Vermouth
$\frac{2}{3}$ Absinthe
Shake well and strain into cocktail glass

McClelland Cocktail
1 dash Absinthe
$\frac{1}{3}$ Curaçao
$\frac{2}{3}$ Sloe Gin
Shake well and strain into cocktail glass

Magnolia Blossom Cocktail
$\frac{1}{4}$ Lemon Juice
$\frac{1}{4}$ cream
$\frac{1}{2}$ Gin
1 dash Grenadine
Shake well and strain into cocktail glass

Mah-Jongg Cocktail
$\frac{1}{6}$ Cointreau
$\frac{1}{6}$ Bacardi Rum
$\frac{2}{3}$ Dry Gin
Shake well and strain into cocktail glass

Cocktails

1 dash Lemon Juice   *Maiden's Blush*
4 dashes Orange Curaçao   *Cocktail (No. 1)*
4 dashes Grenadine
2 oz. Dry Gin
  Shake well and strain into
  cocktail glass

⅓ Absinthe   *Maiden's Blush*
⅔ Dry Gin   *Cocktail (No. 2)*
1 teaspoonful Grenadine
  Shake well and strain into
  cocktail glass

⅛ Orange Juice   *Maiden's Prayer Cocktail*
⅛ Lemon Juice
⅜ Cointreau
⅜ Dry Gin
  Shake well and strain into
  cocktail glass

2 oz. Whisky   *Mamie Taylor Cocktail*
juice of 2 Limes
  Fill tall glass with Ginger
  Ale

1 dash Angostura Bitters   *Manhattan Cocktail*
⅔ Rye Whisky
⅓ Sweet Vermouth
  Stir well and strain into
  cocktail glass. Serve with a
  cherry

Cocktails

Manhattan Cocktail (*Sweet*)	½ Sweet Vermouth ½ Rye Whisky Stir well and strain into cocktail glass
Manhattan Cocktail (*Dry*)	⅓ Dry Vermouth ⅔ Rye Whisky Stir well and strain into cocktail glass
Manyann Cocktail	juice of 1 Lemon 2 dashes Curaçao ½ Gin ½ Caperitif Shake well and strain into Port wineglass
Maragato Cocktail (*Special*)	⅓ Bacardi Rum ⅓ Dry Vermouth ⅓ Sweet Vermouth 1 dash Kirsch juice of ½ Lemon juice of ⅓ Lime a little sugar dissolved in soda-water Shake well and serve in cocktail glass
Margaret Rose Cocktail	⅓ Dry Gin ⅓ Calvados ⅙ Cointreau ⅙ Lemon Juice 1 dash Grenadine Shake well and strain into cocktail glass

Cocktails

2 dessertspoonfuls Orange
   Marmalade
juice of 1 big or 2 small
   Lemons
8 oz. Gin
   Shake carefully and pour
   out, squeezing a piece of
   orange rind into each glass

Marmalade Cocktail
(6 people)

$\frac{1}{3}$ Grand Marnier
$\frac{2}{3}$ Dry Gin
   Shake well and strain into
   cocktail glass

Marny Cocktail

Pour into the shaker 6 oz. of
Gin, 6 of Dry Vermouth,
add a dessertspoonful of
Orange Bitters and 2 of
Curaçao or Maraschino
   Shake and serve with a
   cherry and a piece of lemon
   rind

Martinez Cocktail
(6 people)

$\frac{1}{5}$ Dry Vermouth
$\frac{4}{5}$ Dry Gin
   Stir well with ice and serve
   with a squeeze of lemon
   rind

Martini (Dry) Cocktail

$\frac{1}{7}$ Dry Vermouth
$\frac{6}{7}$ Dry Gin
   Stir well with ice and serve
   with a squeeze of lemon
   rind

Martini (Extra Dry)
Cocktail

93

Cocktails

Martini (Medium)
    Cocktail

$\frac{1}{4}$ Dry Vermouth
$\frac{1}{4}$ Sweet Vermouth
$\frac{1}{2}$ Dry Gin
  Stir well with ice and serve
  with a squeeze of lemon
  rind

Martini (Sweet) Cocktail

$\frac{2}{3}$ Gin
$\frac{1}{3}$ Sweet Vermouth
  Stir well with ice and serve
  with a cherry

Marvel Cocktail

$\frac{3}{4}$ Rum
$\frac{1}{8}$ Sirop-de-Citron
$\frac{1}{8}$ Grenadine
  Shake well and strain into
  cocktail glass

Mary Pickford Cocktail

$\frac{1}{2}$ Bacardi Rum
$\frac{1}{2}$ Pineapple Juice
1 teaspoonful Grenadine
6 drops Maraschino

Maurice Cocktail

1 dash Absinthe
juice of $\frac{1}{4}$ Orange
$\frac{1}{4}$ Sweet Vermouth
$\frac{1}{4}$ Dry Vermouth
$\frac{1}{2}$ Dry Gin
  Shake well and strain into
  cocktail glass

Cocktails

1 dash Clove Syrup
¼ Apricot Brandy
¼ Orange Juice
½ Dry Gin
  Shake well and strain into
  cocktail glass

Mayfair Cocktail

2 dashes Grenadine
2 dashes Absinthe
juice of ¼ Lemon or ½ Lime
1 oz. Bacardi Rum
1 oz. Swedish Punch
  Shake well and strain into
  cocktail glass

Melba Cocktail

⅛ Lemon Juice
⅜ Maraschino
½ Gin
  Shake well and strain into
  cocktail glass

Melon Cocktail

2 dashes Absinthe
2 dashes Angostura Bitters
2 dashes Bénédictine
½ Dry Vermouth
½ Dry Gin
  Stir well and strain into
  cocktail glass. Twist lemon
  peel on top

Merry Widow Cocktail

½ Tequila
½ Pineapple Juice
1 dash Grenadine or Syrup
  Shake well in ice and strain
  into cocktail glass

Mexican Cocktail

95

Cocktails

Mickie Walker Cocktail

1 dash Grenadine
1 dash Lemon Juice
¼ Sweet Vermouth
¾ Scotch Whisky
Shake well and strain into
cocktail glass

Mikado Cocktail

2 dashes Angostura Bitters
2 dashes Crème de Noyau
2 dashes Orgeat Syrup
2 dashes Curaçao
1 oz. Brandy
Shake well and strain into
cocktail glass

Millionaire Cocktail

juice of 1 Lime
1 Dash Grenadine
⅓ Sloe Gin
⅓ Apricot Brandy
⅓ Rum
Shake well and strain into
cocktail glass

Million Dollar Cocktail

1 tablespoonful Pineapple
 Juice
1 teaspoonful Grenadine
white of 1 egg
⅓ Sweet Vermouth
⅔ Gin
Shake well and strain into
medium-size glass

Cocktails

Soak a few sprigs of fresh
mint for two hours in 3 oz.
of White Wine. Add 1 oz.
of Crème de Menthe, 4 oz.
of Gin and 3 more oz. of
White Wine
  Ice and shake thoroughly.
  Serve with a sprig of mint
  arranged in each glass

Mint Cocktail
(6 people)

⅔ Dry Gin
⅙ Lemon Juice
⅙ Crème de Cassis
  Shake well and strain into
  cocktail glass

Mississippi Mule Cocktail

Crush one lump of sugar in a
  little water
Then crush 4 leaves of fresh
  green mint, and add—
1 dash Lemon Juice
4 dashes Orange Juice
2 oz. Gin
  Shake well and strain into
  cocktail glass

Mr. Manhattan Cocktail

¼ Dry Vermouth
¼ Caperitif
½ Dry Gin
  Stir well and strain into
  cocktail glass

Modder River Cocktail

97

Cocktails

Modern Cocktail (No. 1)

1 dash Orange Bitters
2 dashes Rum
1 dash Absinthe
2 dashes Lemon Juice
2 oz. Scotch Whisky
  Shake well and strain into cocktail glass

Modern Cocktail (No. 2)

1 dash Orange Bitters
1 dash Absinthe
1 dash Grenadine
⅓ Scotch Whisky
⅔ Sloe Gin
  Shake well and strain into cocktail glass

Moll Cocktail
(*6 people*)

4 oz. Gin
4 oz. Sloe Gin
4 oz. Dry Vermouth
Add a few drops of Orange Bitters and sugar to taste
  Shake and serve in cocktail glasses

Monkey Gland Cocktail

3 dashes Absinthe
3 dashes Grenadine
⅓ Orange Juice
⅔ Dry Gin
  Shake well and strain into cocktail glass

Cocktails

½ Dry Gin
¼ Lemon Juice
¼ White Crème de Menthe
  Shake well and strain into
  medium-size glass and fill
  up with Champagne

*Monte Carlo Imperial
Cocktail*

3 oz. Grapefruit Juice
4 oz. Gin
1 oz. Kirsch
4 oz. White Wine
  Add ice, shake thoroughly
  and serve, placing in each
  glass a thin shaving of
  lemon peel

*Moonlight Cocktail
(6 people)*

Pour into the shaker 4 oz. of
Brandy, 4 oz. of Quinquina
and 4 oz. of Peach Brandy.
Add 3 dashes of Absinthe
  Shake vigorously and serve

*Moonraker Cocktail
(6 people)*

2 dashes Curaçao
2 dashes Maraschino
2 dashes Orange Bitters
2 dashes Absinthe
½ Brandy
½ Dry Vermouth
  Shake well and strain into
  cocktail glass. Add a cherry
  and squeeze lemon peel on
  top

Morning Cocktail

99

Cocktails

Morning Glory Cocktail

3 dashes Gomme Syrup
2 dashes Curaçao
2 dashes Bitters
1 dash Absinthe
1 oz. Brandy
1 oz. Whisky
1 piece of lemon peel, twisted to express the oil
2 small pieces of ice
Stir thoroughly and remove the ice. Fill the glass with seltzer water or plain soda, and stir with a teaspoon having a little sugar in it

Moulin Rouge Cocktail

3 dashes Grenadine
½ Apricot Brandy
¼ Orange Gin
¼ Lemon Juice
Shake well and strain into cocktail glass

Mountain Cocktail

white of 1 egg
⅙ Lemon Juice
⅙ Dry Vermouth
⅙ Sweet Vermouth
½ Rye Whisky
Shake well and strain into medium-size glass

Cocktails

Mule's Hind Leg Cocktail

⅕ Gin
⅕ Bénédictine
⅕ Applejack
⅕ Maple Syrup
⅕ Apricot Brandy
   Shake well and strain into
   cocktail glass

My Fair Lady Cocktail

½ Gin
¼ Orange Juice
¼ Lemon Juice
1 teaspoonful Fraise Liqueur
white of 1 egg
   Shake well and strain into
   cocktail glass

Napoleon Cocktail

1 dash Fernet Branca
1 dash Curaçao
1 dash Dubonnet
2 oz. Dry Gin
   Shake well and strain into
   cocktail glass. Squeeze lemon
   peel on top

Navy Cocktail

¼ Sweet Vermouth
¾ Bacardi Rum
juice of ¼ Orange
1 dash Angostura Bitters
   Shake well and strain into
   cocktail glass

Cocktails

Negroni Cocktail

$\frac{1}{3}$ Gin
$\frac{1}{3}$ Sweet Vermouth
$\frac{1}{3}$ Campari
Stir well and strain into
cocktail glass. Serve with a
twist of orange rind

Nevada Cocktail

2 oz. Bacardi Rum
juice of $\frac{1}{2}$ Grapefruit
juice of 1 Lime
powdered sugar
1 dash Bitters
Shake well and strain into
cocktail glass

New Arrival Cocktail

2 dashes Crème Yvette
2 dashes Lillet
$\frac{1}{2}$ Orange Bitters
$\frac{1}{2}$ Gin
Stir well and strain into
cocktail glass

Newbury Cocktail

1 piece of Lemon Peel
1 piece of Orange Peel
3 dashes Curaçao
$\frac{1}{2}$ Sweet Vermouth
$\frac{1}{2}$ Dry Gin
Shake well and strain into
cocktail glass

Cocktails

Newton's Special Cocktail

1 dash Angostura Bitters
$\frac{1}{4}$ Cointreau
$\frac{3}{4}$ Brandy
Shake well and strain into
cocktail glass

Cocktails

New York Cocktail

1 lump of sugar
juice of ½ Lime or ¼ Lemon
2 dashes Grenadine
1 piece of Orange Peel
2 oz. Rye Whisky
Shake well and strain into
cocktail glass

Nick's Own Cocktail

1 dash Angostura Bitters
1 dash Absinthe
½ Sweet Vermouth
½ Brandy
Shake well and strain into
cocktail glass. Add cherry
and squeeze lemon peel on
top

Nicolaski Cocktail

2 oz. Brandy
1 slice of lemon with a little
castor sugar spread over it.
Drink Brandy through the
prepared lemon

Night Cap Cocktail

yolk of 1 egg
⅓ Anisette
⅓ Curaçao
⅓ Brandy
Shake well and strain into
cocktail glass

Cocktails

<table>
<tr><td>⅔ Absinthe
⅓ Gin
1 dash Angostura Bitters
1 dash Orange Bitters
1 dash Syrup
Shake well and strain into
cocktail glass</td><td>*Nine-Pick Cocktail*</td></tr>
</table>

⅔ Absinthe
⅓ Gin
1 dash Angostura Bitters
1 dash Orange Bitters
1 dash Syrup
Shake well and strain into
cocktail glass

Nine-Pick Cocktail

1 dash Absinthe
⅙ Dry Gin
⅙ Kirsch
⅔ Dry Vermouth
4 dashes Syrup
Shake well and strain into
cocktail glass

Nineteen Cocktail

¾ Dry Vermouth
¼ Pineapple Juice
Wet edge of glass and dip
in sugar. Shake well and
strain into cocktail glass

North Pole Cocktail

¼ Lemon Juice
¼ Lillet
¼ Cointreau
¼ Brandy
Shake well and strain into
cocktail glass

Odd McIntyre Cocktail

⅓ Bénédictine
⅓ Whisky
⅓ Ginger Ale
Stir well and serve

Oh, Henry! Cocktail

Cocktails

Old Etonian Cocktail

2 dashes Orange Bitters
2 dashes Crème de Noyau
½ Gin
½ Lillet
Shake well and strain into
cocktail glass. Squeeze
orange peel on top

Old Fashioned Cocktail

1 lump of sugar
2 dashes Angostura Bitters
2 oz. Rye Whisky
Crush sugar and Bitters
together, add a lump of ice,
decorate with twist of
lemon peel and slice of
orange using medium-size
glass, and stir well. This
Cocktail can be made with
Brandy, Gin, Rum, etc.,
instead of Rye Whisky

"Old Pal" Cocktail

⅓ Rye Whisky
⅓ Dry Vermouth
⅓ Campari
Stir well and strain into
cocktail glass

Olivette Cocktail

2 dashes Syrup
2 dashes Orange Bitters
3 dashes Absinthe
⅔ Gin
Shake well and strain into
cocktail glass with an olive.
Squeeze lemon peel on top

Cocktails

⅓ Orange Juice   *Olympic Cocktail*
⅓ Curaçao
⅓ Brandy
  Shake well and strain into
  cocktail glass

1 dash Orange Juice   *One Exciting Night*
⅓ Dry Vermouth   *Cocktail*
⅓ Sweet Vermouth
⅓ Gin
  Shake well and strain into
  Port wine glass. Squeeze
  lemon peel on top. Frost
  edge of glass with castor
  sugar

1 dash Angostura Bitters   *Oom Paul Cocktail*
½ Caperitif
½ Apple Brandy
  Shake well and strain into
  cocktail glass

½ Gin   *Opal Cocktail*
⅓ Orange Juice
⅙ Cointreau
a little sugar
  Add a little Orange-flower
  Water. Shake and serve

¼ Grenadine   *Opening Cocktail*
¼ Sweet Vermouth
½ Rye Whisky
  Shake well and strain into
  cocktail glass

Cocktails

Opera Cocktail

$\frac{1}{6}$ Maraschino
$\frac{1}{6}$ Dubonnet
$\frac{2}{3}$ Dry Gin
  Shake well and strain into cocktail glass. Squeeze orange peel on top

Orange Cocktail
(6 people)

Take 3 oz. of fresh Orange Juice, a dessertspoonful of Orange Bitters, 6 oz. of Gin, a dessertspoonful of powdered sugar and $1\frac{1}{2}$ oz. Dry Vermouth. Place the shaker on ice for half an hour, and then shake with 2 or 3 large lumps of ice, so as not to produce too much water. Squeeze a piece of orange peel over each glass and serve

Orange Bloom Cocktail

$\frac{1}{4}$ Sweet Vermouth
$\frac{1}{4}$ Cointreau
$\frac{1}{2}$ Dry Gin
  Shake well and strain into cocktail glass. Add a cherry

Orange Blossom Cocktail

$\frac{1}{2}$ Orange Juice
$\frac{1}{2}$ Dry Gin
  Shake well and strain into cocktail glass

Cocktails

5 oz. Gin
4 oz. Dry Vermouth
2 oz. Sweet Vermouth
Steep in this mixture the
finely-grated rind of 1
orange (carefully removing
all the white pith). Let it
soak for one or two hours,
then add ice and shake.
Rinse out the glasses with
Orange Bitters

Orange Martini Cocktail
(6 people)

½ Rye Whisky
¼ Sweet Vermouth
¼ White Curaçao
juice of ½ Lime
Shake well and strain into
cocktail glass

Oriental Cocktail

1 dash Orange Bitters
1 teaspoonful White Crème
de Menthe
⅓ Sweet Vermouth
⅓ Dry Vermouth
⅓ Gin
Shake well and strain into
cocktail glass

Pall Mall Cocktail

⅓ Bacardi Rum
⅓ Dry Gin
⅓ Pineapple Juice
Shake well in ice and strain
into cocktail glass

Palm Beach Cocktail

Cocktails

Palmer Cocktail

1 dash Lemon Juice
1 dash Angostura Bitters
2 oz. Rye Whisky
Shake well and strain into cocktail glass

Palmetto Cocktail

2 dashes Orange Bitters
½ Sweet Vermouth
½ Rum
Shake well and strain into cocktail glass

Pansy Cocktail

2 dashes Angostura Bitters
6 dashes Grenadine
1 oz. Absinthe
Shake well and strain into cocktail glass

Pansy Blossom Cocktail

2 dashes Angostura Bitters
1 teaspoonful Grenadine
2 oz. Anisette
Shake well and strain into cocktail glass

Pantomime Cocktail

1 dash Orgeat Syrup
1 dash Grenadine
white of 1 egg
1 oz. Dry Vermouth
Shake well and strain into medium-size glass

Cocktails

1 dash Lemon Juice
¼ Orange Juice
½ Gin
¼ Apricot Brandy
   Shake well and strain into
   cocktail glass

Paradise Cocktail

⅓ Dry Vermouth
⅓ Crème de Cassis
⅓ Gin
   Shake well and strain into
   cocktail glass

Parisian Cocktail

⅓ Sweet Cream
⅓ Curaçao
⅓ Rum
   Shake well and strain into
   cocktail glass

Parisian Blonde Cocktail

Put 4 oz. of Gin, 4 oz. of
Sherry, and 4 oz. of
Quinquina in the shaker;
add 2 dashes of Crème de
Cassis and 2 of Abricotine.
   Shake well and serve with a
   cherry and a piece of orange
   peel

Pat's Special Cocktail
(6 people)

½ Rum
½ sweetened Lemon Juice
1 dash Absinthe Bitters
a little nutmeg, grated
   Shake well and strain into
   cocktail glass

Pauline Cocktail

Cocktails

Peggy Cocktail

1 dash Absinthe
1 dash Dubonnet
⅓ Dry Vermouth
⅔ Dry Gin
Shake well and strain into
cocktail glass

Pegu Club Cocktail

1 dash Angostura Bitters
1 dash Orange Bitters
1 teaspoonful Lime Juice
⅓ Curaçao
⅔ Dry Gin
Shake well and strain into
cocktail glass

Perfect Cocktail

⅓ Dry Vermouth
⅓ Sweet Vermouth
⅓ Dry Gin
Shake well and strain into
cocktail glass

Perfect Lady Cocktail

½ Gin
¼ Peach Brandy
¼ Lemon Juice
dash of white of egg
Shake well and strain into
cocktail glass

Peter Pan Cocktail

¼ Peach Bitters
¼ Orange Juice
¼ Dry Vermouth
¼ Dry Gin
Shake well and strain into
cocktail glass

Cocktails

Peto Cocktail

juice of ¼ Orange
¼ Dry Vermouth
¼ Sweet Vermouth
½ Gin
2 dashes Maraschino
Shake well and strain into
cocktail glass

*Philadelphia Scotchman
Cocktail*

2 oz. Applejack
2 oz. Port
juice of 1 Orange
Place in tumbler and fill up
with Ginger Ale

Philomel Cocktail
(6 people)

5 oz. Sherry
2 oz. Rum
2½ oz. Quinquina
3 oz. Orange Juice
Give one grind of the
peppermill over this. Shake:
serve!

Phoebe Snow Cocktail

1 dash Absinthe
½ Brandy
½ Dubonnet
Shake well and strain into
cocktail glass

Piccad Cocktail

3 dashes Angostura Bitters
½ Capertitif
½ Dry Gin
Shake well with two or
three pieces of lemon rind
and strain

113

Cocktails

Piccadilly Cocktail

1 dash Absinthe
1 dash Grenadine
⅓ Dry Vermouth
⅔ Dry Gin
Shake well and strain into
cocktail glass

Picon Cocktail

½ Sweet Vermouth
½ Amer Picon
Shake well and strain into
cocktail glass

Picon and Grenadine
Cocktail

1 oz. Amer Picon
½ oz. Grenadine
Use medium-size glass and
fill with soda water.

Pineapple Cocktail
(6 people)

First take 2 oz. of fresh
Pineapple Juice. Soak the
fruit from which this juice
has been extracted for 2
hours in 4 oz. of Dry White
Wine. Mix these together,
adding as well the juice of
¼ lemon, and pour it all in
the shaker with 6 oz. of
Sherry. Stand the shaker in
ice, but do not put any ice
into the mixture. Shake,
strain and serve with a
small piece of Pineapple in
each glass. This is a very
mild cocktail

Cocktails

juice of ¼ Lemon
½ Sloe Gin
½ Crème Yvette
  Shake well and strain into
  cocktail glass

Ping-Pong Cocktail

Carefully shake together 6 oz.
of Sloe Gin and 6 oz. of
Sweet Vermouth, with
½ dessertspoonful of
Angostura Bitters and a
dessertspoonful of sugar
syrup or Curaçao
  Serve with a
  cherry and a piece of lemon
  rind

*Ping-Pong Special
Cocktail
(6 people)*

½ Gin
¼ Grenadine
¼ Sirop-de-Citron
white of 1 egg
  Shake well and strain into
  medium-size glass

Pink Baby Cocktail

1 dash Angostura Bitters
2 oz. Gin
  Shake well and strain into
  cocktail glass

Pink Gin Cocktail

white of 1 egg
1 oz. Grenadine
2 oz. Gin
  Shake well and strain into
  medium-size glass

Pink Lady Cocktail

Cocktails

Pink Pearl Cocktail
(6 people)

Take 3 oz. of Grapefruit Juice, a dessertspoonful of Lemon Juice, ½ dessertspoonful of Grenadine Syrup, and the white of 1 egg. Add plenty of crushed ice and shake thoroughly

Pink Rose Cocktail

white of 1 egg
1 teaspoonful Grenadine
1 teaspoonful Lemon Juice
1 teaspoonful sweet cream
⅔ Dry Gin
Shake well and strain into cocktail glass

Pinky Cocktail

white of 1 egg
½ Grenadine
½ Dry Gin
Shake well and strain into cocktail glass

Plain Sherry Cocktail
(6 people)

Pour into the shaker 12 oz. of Sherry, a few drops of Absinthe Bitters, and a few drops of Maraschino
Shake very thoroughly and serve

Cocktails

11 oz. Dry Vermouth
1 teaspoonful Absinthe
  Bitters
1 teaspoonful Maraschino
  Shake very thoroughly and
  serve with a cherry

Plain Vermouth Cocktail
(6 people)

1 dash Lemon Juice
½ Orange Juice
½ Rum
  Shake well and strain into
  cocktail glass

Planter's Cocktail

Use small tumbler
1 dash Angostura Bitters
1 teaspoonful Green Crème
  de Menthe
1 oz. Dry Gin
  Stir, add cracked ice, and
  fill with Ginger Beer.
  Decorate with cherry, slice
  of apple and sprig of mint
  on top

Playing Fields Cocktail

⅓ Sweet Vermouth
⅓ Dry Vermouth
⅓ Dry Gin
1 slice of Pineapple
  Shake well and strain into
  cocktail glass

Plaza Cocktail

117

Cocktails

Poet's Dream Cocktail

⅓ Dry Vermouth
⅔ Dry Gin
2 dashes Orange Bitters
2 dashes Bénédictine
Shake well and strain into
cocktail glass

Poker Cocktail

½ Sweet Vermouth
½ Bacardi Rum
Shake well and strain into
cocktail glass

Polo Cocktail

juice of ¼ Lemon or ½ Lime
⅓ Sweet Vermouth
⅓ Dry Vermouth
⅓ Dry Gin
Shake well and strain into
cocktail glass

Poop Deck Cocktail

½ Blackberry Brandy
¼ Port Wine
¼ Brandy
Shake well and strain into
cocktail glass

Poppy Cocktail

⅓ Crème de Cacao
⅔ Dry Gin
Shake well and strain into
cocktail glass

Cocktails

½ Vodka
⅙ Orange Juice
⅛ Apricot Brandy
$\frac{1}{12}$ Grenadine
$\frac{1}{12}$ Yolk of egg
  Shake well and strain into
  cocktail glass

Porte Cochere Cocktail

1 measure of Port
white of 1 egg
  Shake well in ice and strain
  into small glass. Grate
  nutmeg on top

Porto Rico Cocktail

1 dash Brandy
2 oz. Port Wine
  Stir slightly in ice and
  strain. Squeeze orange peel
  on top

*Port Wine Cocktail
(No. 1)*

1 dash Angostura Bitters
1 dash Orange Bitters
2 dashes Curaçao
2 oz. Port Wine
  Stir well and strain into
  Port wineglass

*Port Wine Cocktail
(No. 2)*

2 dashes Grenadine
juice of ¼ Orange
2 oz. Bacardi Rum
  Shake well and strain into
  cocktail glass

President Cocktail

Cocktails

Presto Cocktail

1 dash Absinthe
1/6 Orange Juice
1/6 Sweet Vermouth
2/3 Brandy
Shake well and strain into
cocktail glass

Princess Mary Cocktail

1/3 Crème de Cacao
1/3 sweet cream
1/3 Dry Gin
Shake well and strain into
cocktail glass

Princeton Cocktail

2 dashes Orange Bitters
1/3 Port Wine
2/3 Gin
Stir well and strain into
cocktail glass. Squeeze
lemon peel on top

Pruneaux Cocktail
(6 people)

4 oz. Gin
4 oz. Sherry
2 oz. Syrup of Prunes
2 oz. strained Orange Juice
Shake thoroughly in cracked
ice and serve

Puritan Cocktail

1/2 Gin
1/2 Lillet
2 dashes Orange Juice
1 dash Apricot Brandy
Shake well and strain into
cocktail glass. Squeeze
lemon peel on top

Cocktails

Quaker's Cocktail

⅓ Brandy
⅓ Rum
⅙ Lemon Juice
⅙ Raspberry Syrup
Shake well and strain into
cocktail glass

Quarter Deck Cocktail

1 teaspoonful Lime Juice
⅓ Sherry
⅔ Rum
Shake well and strain into
cocktail glass

Queen Elizabeth Cocktail

1 dash Absinthe
¼ Lemon Juice
¼ Cointreau
½ Dry Gin
Shake well and strain into
cocktail glass

Queen's Cocktail

½ slice of crushed Pineapple
¼ Dry Vermouth
¼ Sweet Vermouth
½ Gin
Shake well and strain into
cocktail glass

Cocktails

Raspberry Cocktail
(6 people)

Slightly bruise a cupful of fresh raspberries and add 4 oz. of Gin. Soak for two hours and strain. Complete the mixture by adding 1 oz. of Kirsch and 4 oz. of any White Wine which is not too sweet, such as Moselle, Graves or Chablis. Ice; shake; put a raspberry in each glass and serve. This is a delightfully refreshing summer cocktail

Rattlesnake Cocktail
(6 people)

8 oz. Rye Whisky
whites of 2 eggs
2 oz. sweetened Lemon
  Juice
a few dashes Absinthe
  Shake very thoroughly and
  serve by straining it
  through a fine sieve

Ray Long Cocktail

1 dash Angostura Bitters
4 dashes Absinthe
⅓ Sweet Vermouth
⅔ Brandy
  Shake well and strain into
  cocktail glass

Cocktails

juice of ½ Orange   *Raymond Hitch Cocktail*
1 dash Orange Bitters
1 slice of Pineapple
2 oz. Sweet Vermouth
  Shake well and strain into
  cocktail glass

¼ Bacardi Rum   *Red Flag Cocktail*
¼ Dry Gin
¼ Lemon Juice
¼ Pineapple Juice
1 dash Grenadine or Syrup
  Shake well and strain into
  cocktail glass

1 dash Orange Bitters   *Reform Cocktail*
⅓ Dry Vermouth
⅔ Sherry
  Stir well and strain into
  cocktail glass. Add
  a cherry

¼ Lemon Juice   *Resolute Cocktail*
¼ Apricot Brandy
½ Dry Gin
  Shake well and strain into
  cocktail glass

½ Gin   *Reverie Cocktail*
¼ Dubonnet
¼ Van der Hum
1 dash Orange Juice
  Shake well and strain into
  cocktail glass

Cocktails

Richmond Cocktail

$\frac{1}{3}$ Lillet
$\frac{2}{3}$ Gin
Stir well and strain into
cocktail glass. Squeeze
lemon peel on top

Rob Roy Cocktail

1 dash Angostura Bitters
$\frac{1}{3}$ Sweet Vermouth
$\frac{2}{3}$ Scotch Whisky
Stir well and strain into
cocktail glass

Robson Cocktail

$\frac{1}{8}$ Lemon Juice
$\frac{1}{8}$ Orange Juice
$\frac{1}{4}$ Grenadine
$\frac{1}{2}$ Rum
Shake well and strain into
cocktail glass

Roc-a-Coe Cocktail

$\frac{1}{2}$ Sherry
$\frac{1}{2}$ Dry Gin
Stir well and strain into
cocktail glass. Add a cherry

Rock and Rye Cocktail

2 oz. Rye Whisky
Dissolve 1 piece of Rock
Candy in it
juice of 1 Lemon can be
added if desired

Cocktails

1 dash Bénédictine
¼ Dry Vermouth
¼ Sweet Vermouth
½ Dry Gin
Shake well and strain into
cocktail glass

Rolls Royce Cocktail

⅓ Sweet Vermouth
⅓ Dry Vermouth
⅙ Campari
⅙ Gin
1 dash Strega
Stir well and strain into
cocktail glass. Add a
squeeze of lemon peel

Roma Cocktail

1 dash Lemon Juice
4 dashes Grenadine
¼ Apricot Brandy
¼ Dry Vermouth
½ Dry Gin
Stir well and strain into
cocktail glass

Rose Cocktail
(ENGLISH)

¼ Cherry Brandy
¼ Dry Vermouth
½ Dry Gin
Stir well and strain into
cocktail glass

Rose Cocktail
(FRENCH)

2 dashes Grenadine
⅓ Dry Vermouth
⅔ Dry Gin
Shake well and strain into
cocktail glass. Squeeze
lemon peel on top

Roselyn Cocktail

Cocktails

Roulette Cocktail

$\frac{1}{4}$ Swedish Punch
$\frac{1}{4}$ Bacardi Rum
$\frac{1}{2}$ Apple Brandy
Shake well and strain into
cocktail glass

Royal Cocktail

$\frac{1}{3}$ Gin
$\frac{1}{3}$ Dry Vermouth
$\frac{1}{3}$ Cherry Brandy
1 dash Maraschino
Shake well and strain into
cocktail glass, with a cherry

Royal Arrival Cocktail

$\frac{1}{2}$ Gin
$\frac{1}{4}$ Lemon
$\frac{1}{8}$ Crème de Noyaux
$\frac{1}{8}$ Kummel
1 dash Blue Vegetable Extract
a little white of egg
Shake well and strain into
cocktail glass

Royal Clover Club
Cocktail

juice of $\frac{1}{2}$ Lemon
1 tablespoonful Grenadine
yolk of 1 egg
2 oz. Gin
Shake well and strain into
medium-size glass

Royal Smile Cocktail

juice of $\frac{1}{4}$ Lemon
$\frac{1}{4}$ Grenadine
$\frac{1}{2}$ Applejack
$\frac{1}{4}$ Dry Gin
Shake well and strain into
cocktail glass

Cocktails

½ Orange Juice
¼ Peach Brandy
¼ Kirsch
Shake well and strain into
champagne cocktail glass.
Top up with Champagne

Royal Wedding Cocktail

½ Lillet
¼ Brandy
¼ Orange Juice
2 dashes Grenadine
Shake well and strain into
cocktail glass

Roy Howard Cocktail

¼ Sweet Vermouth
¾ Rum
Stir well and strain into
cocktail glass

Rum Cocktail

2 dashes Orange Bitters
2 dashes Syrup
3 dashes Blackberry Brandy
2 oz. Rye Whisky
Shake well and strain into
cocktail glass

Russell House Cocktail

Russian Cocktail

⅓ Crème de Cacao
⅓ Dry Gin
⅓ Vodka
Shake well, strain into
cocktail glass, and tossitoff
quickski

Cocktails

Rusty Nail Cocktail

½ Scotch Whisky
½ Drambuie
Stir well and strain into
cocktail glass. Can be served
on the rocks

Rye Whisky Cocktail

1 dash Angostura Bitters
4 dashes Syrup
2 oz. Rye Whisky
Stir well and strain into
cocktail glass. Add a cherry

St. Germain Cocktail

juice of ½ Lemon
juice of ¼ Grapefruit
White of 1 egg
1 oz. Green Chartreuse
Shake well and strain into
cocktail glass

St. Mark Cocktail

⅙ Groseille
⅓ Gin
⅙ Cherry Brandy
⅓ Dry Vermouth
Shake well and strain into
cocktail glass

Salomé Cocktail

⅓ Dry Vermouth
⅓ Dry Gin
⅓ Dubonnet
Shake well and strain into
cocktail glass

Cocktails

⅔ Dry Gin   *Salutation Cocktail*
⅓ Bénédictine
1 dash Cherry Brandy
  Stir well and strain into
  cocktail glass. Serve with a
  cherry

¼ Cointreau   *Sanctuary Cocktail*
¼ Amer Picon
½ Dubonnet
  Shake well and strain into
  cocktail glass

1 teaspoonful Green   *Sand-Martin Cocktail*
  Chartreuse
½ Sweet Vermouth
½ Dry Gin
  Shake well and strain into
  cocktail glass

2 dashes Grenadine   *Santiago Cocktail*
2 dashes Lemon Juice
2 oz. Bacardi Rum
  Shake well and strain into
  cocktail glass

2 dashes Maraschino   *Saratoga Cocktail*
2 dashes Angostura Bitters
¼ slice of Pineapple
2 oz. Brandy
  Shake well and strain,
  adding a little soda water

Cocktails

Satan's Whiskers Cocktail
(STRAIGHT)

Of Sweet Vermouth, Dry Vermouth, Gin and Orange Juice, two parts each; of Grand Marnier one part; Orange Bitters, a dash
Shake well and strain into cocktail glass

Cocktails

For the Grand Marnier in the foregoing Cocktail,
substitute the same quantity
  of Orange Curaçao
  Shake well and strain into
  cocktail glass

Satan's Whiskers Cocktail
(CURLED)

1 dash Apricot Brandy
1 dash Absinthe
½ Apple Brandy
½ Brandy
  Stir well and squeeze orange
  peel on top

Saucy Sue Cocktail

1 dash Absinthe
2 dashes Grenadine
⅓ Dry Vermouth
⅔ Dry Gin
  Shake well and strain into
  cocktail glass. Squeeze
  lemon peel on top

Savoy Special Cocktail

½ Sloe Gin
½ Applejack
  Shake well and strain into
  cocktail glass

Savoy Tango Cocktail

1 lump of sugar
1 dash Angostura Bitters
2 oz. Rye Whisky
  Stir well and strain into
  another glass that has been
  cooled, add 1 dash Absinthe
  and squeeze lemon peel on top

Sazerac Cocktail

Cocktails

Scoff-Law Cocktail

1 dash Orange Bitters
⅓ Rye Whisky
⅓ Dry Vermouth
⅙ Lemon Juice
⅙ Grenadine
Shake well and strain into
cocktail glass

Scotch Kilt Cocktail

⅔ Scotch Whisky
⅓ Drambuie
2 dashes Orange Bitters
twist of orange peel
Stir well and strain into
cocktail glass

Scotch Mist Cocktail

Shake 2 oz. of Scotch Whisky
with crushed ice and pour
unstrained into a champagne
glass. Add a twist of lemon
peel and serve with straws

Screwdriver Cocktail

⅓ Vodka
⅔ Orange Juice
Shake well and strain into
medium-size glass. Add ice
and a slice of orange

Self-Starter Cocktail

⅛ Apricot Brandy
⅜ Lillet
½ Dry Gin
2 dashes Absinthe
Shake well and strain into
cocktail glass

Cocktails

3 dashes Maraschino   *Sensation Cocktail*
3 sprigs fresh mint
¼ Lemon Juice
¾ Dry Gin
  Shake well and strain into
  cocktail glass

juice of ½ Lemon or 1 Lime   *September Morn Cocktail*
1 tablespoonful Grenadine
white of 1 egg
2 oz. Bacardi Rum
  Shake well and strain into
  medium size-glass

1 dash Angostura Bitters   *Seventh Heaven Cocktail*
2 dashes Maraschino
½ Caperitif
½ Dry Gin
  Stir well and strain into
  cocktail glass. Squeeze orange
  peel on top. Add a cherry

½ Sweet Vermouth   *Sevilla Cocktail (No. 1)*
½ Bacardi Rum
1 piece of Orange Peel
  Shake well and strain into
  cocktail glass

½ teaspoonful powdered sugar *Sevilla Cocktail (No. 2)*
1 egg
½ Port Wine
½ Bacardi Rum
  Shake well and strain into
  cocktail glass

Cocktails

"S.G." Cocktail

1 teaspoonful Grenadine
⅓ Rye Whisky
⅓ Lemon Juice
⅓ Orange Juice
Shake well and strain into
cocktail glass

Shamrock Cocktail

3 dashes Green Crème de
  Menthe
3 dashes Green Chartreuse
½ Dry Vermouth
½ Irish Whiskey
Shake well and strain into
cocktail glass

Shanghai Cocktail

2 dashes Grenadine
⅜ Lemon Juice
⅛ Anisette
½ Rum
Shake well and strain into
cocktail glass

Sharky Punch Cocktail

1 teaspoonful syrup
¼ Rye Whisky
¾ Apple Brandy
Shake well and strain into
medium-size glass and fill
with soda-water

Sherry Cocktail

4 dashes Orange Bitters
4 dashes Dry Vermouth
2 oz. Sherry
Stir well and strain into
cocktail glass

Cocktails

Sherry and Egg Cocktail

Place an egg in a large Port
wineglass, taking care not
to break the yolk. Fill glass
with Sherry

Sherry Twist Cocktail
(No. 1)
(6 people)

2 oz. Brandy
2 oz. Dry Vermouth
6 oz. Sherry
1½ oz. Cointreau
½ oz. Lemon Juice
1 small piece of cinnamon
   Shake well and strain into
   cocktail glasses

Sherry Twist Cocktail
(No. 2)
(6 people)

Take the juice of 1 Orange,
4 oz. of Whisky, 5 oz. of
Sherry and 1 oz. of
Cointreau. Add 2 cloves,
squeeze in the juice of
¼ Lemon, and add half a
turn of the peppermill. Fill
the shaker with cracked ice
   Shake and serve

Ship Cocktail

⅜ Sherry
⅛ Whisky
⅛ Rum
⅛ Prune Syrup
1 dash Orange Bitters
a little sugar if desired
   Shake well and strain into
   cocktail glass

Cocktails

Sidecar Cocktail

¼ Lemon Juice
¼ Cointreau
½ Brandy
Shake well and strain into cocktail glass

Silver Cocktail

2 dashes Maraschino
2 dashes Orange Bitters
½ Dry Vermouth
½ Dry Gin
Shake well and strain into cocktail glass

Silver Bells Cocktail

⅓ Bacardi Rum
⅓ Lemon Juice
⅓ Gin
2 dashes Crème de Noyau
Shake well and strain.
Before pouring this cocktail run a piece of lemon rind round the rim of the glass and dip the glass upside down in powdered sugar

Silver Bullet Cocktail

½ Gin
¼ Lemon Juice
¼ Kummel
Shake well and strain into cocktail glass

Cocktails

juice of ¼ Lemon   *Silver King Cocktail*
1 teaspoonful sugar
2 dashes Orange Bitters
white of 1 egg
2 oz. Gin
  Shake well and strain into
  cocktail glass

½ Vanilla Ice Cream   *Silver Stallion Cocktail*
½ Gin
Fill with Silver Fizz, see
  p. 207

½ Kummel   *Silver Streak Cocktail*
½ Dry Gin
  Shake well and strain into
  cocktail glass

1 teaspoonful Grenadine   *Sir Walter Cocktail*
1 teaspoonful Curaçao   *(commonly known as*
1 teaspoonful Lemon Juice   *the "Swalter")*
⅓ Brandy
⅓ Rum
  Shake well and strain into
  cocktail glass

2 oz. Brandy   *Sleepy Head Cocktail*
1 piece of orange peel
4 leaves of fresh mint
  Put in long tumbler and fill
  with Ginger Ale

Cocktails

Sloe Gin Cocktail

$\frac{1}{4}$ Dry Vermouth
$\frac{1}{4}$ Sweet Vermouth
$\frac{1}{2}$ Sloe Gin
Stir well and strain into
cocktail glass

Sloe Measure Cocktail

$\frac{1}{2}$ Sloe Gin
$\frac{1}{2}$ Lillet
2 dashes Orange Bitters
2 dashes Crème de Noyaux
Stir well with ice

Sloeberry Cocktail

1 dash Angostura Bitters
1 dash Orange Bitters
2 oz. Sloe Gin
Shake well and strain into
cocktail glass

Smiler Cocktail

1 dash Angostura Bitters
1 dash Orange Juice
$\frac{1}{4}$ Sweet Vermouth
$\frac{1}{4}$ Dry Vermouth
$\frac{1}{2}$ Dry Gin
Shake well and strain into
cocktail glass

Snicker Cocktail

white of 1 egg
2 dashes Maraschino
1 teaspoonful syrup
1 dash Orange Bitters
$\frac{1}{3}$ Dry Vermouth
$\frac{2}{3}$ Dry Gin
Shake well and strain into
medium-size glass

138

Cocktails

⅙ Crème de Violette   *Snowball Cocktail*
⅙ White Crème de Menthe
⅙ Anisette
⅙ sweet cream
⅓ Dry Gin
  Shake well and strain into
  cocktail glass

⅓ Dry Vermouth   *Snyder Cocktail*
⅔ Dry Gin
3 dashes Curaçao
  Shake well and strain into
  cocktail glass. Twist orange
  peel on top

¼ Sweet Vermouth   *Soho Cocktail*
½ Chianti
¼ Grapefruit Juice
  Shake well in ice and strain
  into cocktail glass

1 dash Lemon Juice   *Sonora Cocktail*
2 dashes Apricot Brandy
½ Applejack
½ Bacardi Rum
  Shake well and strain into
  cocktail glass

½ Gin   *Sonza's Wilson Cocktail*
½ Cherry Brandy
4 dashes Lemon Juice or
  Lime Juice
4 dashes Grenadine
  Shake well and strain into
  cocktail glass

Cocktails

So-So Cocktail

⅙ Grenadine
⅙ Apple Brandy
⅓ Sweet Vermouth
⅓ Dry Gin
Shake well and strain into
cocktail glass

Soul Kiss Cocktail
(No. 1)

⅙ Orange Juice
⅙ Dubonnet
⅓ Dry Vermouth
⅓ Sweet Vermouth
Shake well and strain into
cocktail glass

Soul Kiss Cocktail
(No. 2)

⅙ Orange Juice
⅙ Dubonnet
⅓ Dry Vermouth
⅓ Rye Whisky
1 slice of Orange
Shake well and strain into
cocktail glass

Southern Gin Cocktail

2 dashes Curaçao
2 dashes Orange Bitters
2 oz. Dry Gin
Shake well and strain into
cocktail glass

South Side Cocktail

juice of ½ Lemon
½ tablespoonful powdered
   sugar
2 sprigs fresh mint
2 oz. Dry Gin
Shake well and strain into
medium-size glass. Add a
dash of syphon soda water

Cocktails

1 oz. Ice Cream
2 dashes Maraschino
2 dashes Curaçao
2 dashes Brandy
  Stir well together in medium-
  size glass and fill with
  Champagne. Add slice of
  pineapple or orange, a
  cherry or strawberry

*Soyer-au Champagne
Cocktail*

10 oz. Rum
½ oz. Curaçao
  Pour into shaker, add a large
  quantity of ice, and shake
  thoroughly. Grate a little
  nutmeg over each glass and
  serve

*Spanish Town Cocktail
(6 people)*

1 dash Absinthe
½ Applejack (known in
  America as "Jersey
  Lightning")
½ Brandy
  Shake well and strain into
  cocktail glass. Serve very cold

Special Rough Cocktail

1 dash Angostura Bitters
1 dash Orange Juice
⅛ Apricot Brandy
⅔ Dry Gin
  Shake well and strain into
  cocktail glass. Add a cherry
  and squeeze orange peel on
  top

Spencer Cocktail

141

Cocktails

Spion Kop Cocktail

½ Dry Vermouth
½ Caperitif
Stir well and strain into cocktail glass

Spokane Cocktail

⅓ Lemon Juice
⅔ Dry Gin
4 dashes Sugar Syrup
white of 1 egg
Shake well and strain into medium-size glass

Spring Cocktail

⅗ Gin
⅕ Quinquina
⅕ Bénédictine
Before shaking add a dash of Bitters. Serve with an olive

Springbok Cocktail

⅓ Sherry
⅓ Lillet
⅓ Van der Hum
2 dashes Orange Bitters
Stir well and strain into cocktail glass

Spring Feeling Cocktail

¼ Lemon Juice
¼ Green Chartreuse
½ Gin
Shake well and strain into cocktail glass

Cocktails

⅓ Drambuie
⅓ Scotch Whisky
⅓ Orange Juice
  Shake well and strain into
  cocktail glass

St. Andrew's Cocktail

⅙ Lemon Juice
⅙ Grenadine
⅓ Gin
⅓ Rum
  Shake well and strain into
  cocktail glass

Stanley Cocktail

1 teaspoonful Grapefruit
  Juice
1 dash Sweet Vermouth
1 dash Dry Vermouth
½ Apple Brandy
½ Dry Gin
  Shake well and strain into
  cocktail glass

Star Cocktail (No. 1)

½ Sweet Vermouth
½ Applejack
  Shake well and strain into
  cocktail glass

Star Cocktail (No. 2)

½ Dry Gin
¼ Lemon Juice
¼ Green Crème de Menthe
  Shake well and strain into
  cocktail glass

Starboard Light Cocktail

Cocktails

Stone Fence Cocktail

1 lump of ice
2 dashes Angostura Bitters
2 oz. Scotch Whisky
  Use long tumbler and fill
  with soda-water

Strawberry Cocktail
(*6 people*)

Pass 1 lb. of Strawberries
through a hair-sieve and
pour the juice into the
shaker, together with the
juice of 1 Orange and a
dash of Whisky. Add a few
pieces of ice
  Shake carefully and serve

Suisse Cocktail

white of 1 egg
4 dashes Anisette
1 oz. Absinthe
syrup or sugar can be used
  instead of Anisette
  Shake well and strain into
  medium-size glass

Summertime Cocktail

$\frac{3}{4}$ Gin
$\frac{1}{4}$ Sirop-de-Citron
  Shake well and strain into
  medium-size glass

Cocktails

Place in a large glass the
thinly-cut rind of an orange
or a tangerine. Add a
teaspoonful of Peach
Preserve, and a large
apricot and its crushed
kernel. Pour on 2 oz. of
Brandy and $\frac{1}{4}$ oz. of Kirsch.
Let this soak for 2 hours.
Then transfer the mixture
to the shaker and add 1 oz.
of White Wine, 3 oz. of Gin
and 2 oz. of Dry Vermouth.
Add plenty of ice
  Shake and serve

Sunshine Cocktail

juice of $\frac{1}{4}$ Lemon
2 dashes Crème de Cassis
$\frac{1}{2}$ Dry Vermouth
$\frac{1}{2}$ Bacardi Rum
  Shake well and strain into
  cocktail glass

Swan Cocktail

$\frac{1}{2}$ Dry Vermouth
$\frac{1}{2}$ Dry Gin
3 drops Lime Juice or
  Lemon Juice
1 dash Angostura Bitters
  Shake well and strain into
  cocktail glass

145

Cocktails

Swazi Freeze Cocktail

1 dash Peach Brandy
⅓ Rye Whisky
⅔ Caperitif
Stir well and strain into
cocktail glass

Sweet Patotie Cocktail

¼ Orange Juice
¼ Cointreau
½ Dry Gin
Shake well and strain into
cocktail glass

Swizzles Cocktail

juice of 1 Lime
1 dash Angostura Bitters
2 oz. Gin
1 teaspoonful sugar
Stir with swizzle stick in
tumbler with cracked ice
until foaming

Tanglefoot Cocktail

⅙ Orange Juice
⅙ Lemon Juice
⅓ Bacardi Rum
⅓ Swedish Punch
Shake well and strain into
cocktail glass

Tango Cocktail

2 dashes Curaçao
juice of ¼ Orange
¼ Dry Vermouth
¼ Sweet Vermouth
½ Dry Gin
Shake well and strain into
cocktail glass

Cocktails

¼ Sweet Vermouth   *Tavern Cocktail*
¼ Dry Vermouth
½ Dry Gin
Lime Juice
1 dash Absinthe
   Shake well and strain into
   cocktail glass

1 piece of Orange Peel   *Temptation Cocktail*
1 piece of Lemon Peel
2 dashes Dubonnet
2 dashes Absinthe
2 dashes Curaçao
2 oz. Rye Whisky
   Shake well and strain into
   cocktail glass

½ Port Wine   *Tempter Cocktail*
½ Apricot Brandy
   Shake well and strain into
   cocktail glass

½ Dry Gin   *The Ashes Cocktail*
¼ Lemon Juice
2 dashes Yellow Chartreuse
¼ Marnique
   Shake well and strain into
   cocktail glass. Serve with
   cherry on stick across top of
   glass

Cocktails

The New Savoyard Cocktail

½ Kirsch
¼ Cherry Brandy
¼ Crème de Noyau
3 dashes Orange Bitters
Stir well and strain into cocktail glass

Third Degree Cocktail

⅔ Gin
⅓ Dry Vermouth
4 dashes Absinthe
Shake well and strain into old-fashioned whisky glass

Third Rail Cocktail (No. 1)

1 dash White Mint
1 dash Curaçao
2 oz. Dry Vermouth
Shake well and strain into cocktail glass

Third Rail Cocktail (No. 2)

1 dash Absinthe
⅓ Bacardi Rum
⅓ Apple Brandy
⅓ Brandy
Shake well and strain into cocktail glass

"This is It" Cocktail

¼ Lemon Juice
¼ Cointreau
½ Gin
white of 1 egg
Shake well in ice, strain into medium-size glass

Cocktails

2 dashes Angostura Bitters
½ Sweet Vermouth
½ Scotch Whisky
   Shake well and strain into
   cocktail glass

Thistle Cocktail

1 teaspoonful Grenadine
1 dash Lemon Juice
⅔ Brandy
⅓ Bacardi Rum
   Shake well and strain into
   cocktail glass

Three Miller Cocktail

3 slices of Orange
⅓ Dry Vermouth
⅔ Dry Gin
   Shake well and strain into
   cocktail glass

Three Stripes Cocktail

1 teaspoonful Gomme Syrup
yolk of 1 egg
2 oz. Brandy
1 sprinkle of Cayenne pepper
   Shake well and strain into
   cocktail glass

Thunder Cocktail

Cocktails

Thunder and Lightning Cocktail

yolk of 1 egg
1 teaspoonful powdered
 sugar
2 oz. Brandy
 Shake well and strain into
 medium-size glass, a dash
 of cayenne pepper on top

Tinton Cocktail

⅓ Port Wine
⅔ Applejack
 Shake well and strain into
 cocktail glass

Tipperary Cocktail (No. 1)

⅓ Sweet Vermouth
⅓ Green Chartreuse
⅓ Irish Whiskey
 Shake well and strain into
 cocktail glass

Tipperary Cocktail (No. 2)

⅙ Orange Juice
⅙ Grenadine
⅓ Dry Vermouth
⅓ Dry Gin
2 sprigs green mint
 Shake well and strain into
 cocktail glass

Cocktails

½ Rye Whisky
½ Absinthe
Shake well and strain into
cocktail glass

T.N.T. Cocktail

Cocktails

Toby Special Cocktail

$\frac{1}{4}$ Lemon Juice
$\frac{1}{4}$ Grenadine or Sugar Syrup
$\frac{1}{4}$ Apricot Brandy
$\frac{1}{4}$ Bacardi Rum
Shake well in ice and strain into cocktail glass

Toddy's Cocktail

Dissolve 1 lump of sugar in water. Use 2 oz. of any Spirit desired, and 1 lump of ice
Use medium-size glass and stir well

Tom and Jerry Cocktail

1 egg
1 oz. Rum
1 tablespoonful powdered sugar
1 oz. Brandy
Beat up yolk and white of egg separately, then mix together. Use stem glass or china mug; add the spirits, fill with boiling water, and grate nutmeg on top

Torpedo Cocktail

1 dash Gin
$\frac{1}{3}$ Brandy
$\frac{2}{3}$ Apple Brandy
Shake well and strain into cocktail glass

Cocktails

Transvaal Cocktail
3 dashes Orange Bitters
½ Gin
½ Caperitif
Stir well and strain into
cocktail glass

Treble Chance Cocktail
⅓ Scotch Whisky
⅓ Dry Vermouth
⅓ Cointreau
Stir in ice and strain into
cocktail glass

Trilby Cocktail
2 dashes Absinthe
2 dashes Orange Bitters
⅓ Parfait Amour Liqueur
⅓ Scotch Whisky
⅓ Sweet Vermouth
Shake well and strain into
cocktail glass

Trocadero Cocktail
1 dash Orange Bitters
1 dash Grenadine
½ Dry Vermouth
½ Sweet Vermouth
Stir well and strain into
cocktail glass. Add a cherry
and squeeze lemon peel on top

Tropical Cocktail
1 dash Angostura Bitters
1 dash Orange Bitters
⅓ Crème de Cacao
⅓ Maraschino
⅓ Dry Vermouth
Shake well and strain into
cocktail glass

Cocktails

Tulip Cocktail

$\frac{1}{6}$ Lemon Juice
$\frac{1}{6}$ Apricot Brandy
$\frac{1}{3}$ Sweet Vermouth
$\frac{1}{3}$ Apple Brandy
Shake well and strain into
cocktail glass

Tunny Cocktail

$\frac{1}{3}$ Dry Gin
$\frac{2}{3}$ Applejack
2 dashes Absinthe
1 dash Syrup
Stir well and strain into
cocktail glass

Turf Cocktail

2 dashes Orange Bitters
2 dashes Maraschino
2 dashes Absinthe
$\frac{1}{2}$ Dry Vermouth
$\frac{1}{2}$ Gin
Shake well and strain into
cocktail glass

Tuxedo Cocktail

1 dash Maraschino
1 dash Absinthe
2 dashes Orange Bitters
$\frac{1}{2}$ Dry Gin
$\frac{1}{2}$ Dry Vermouth
Shake well and strain into
cocktail glass. Add a cherry.
Squeeze lemon peel on top

Cocktails

½ Bacardi Rum   *Twelve Miles Out Cocktail*
⅓ Swedish Punch
⅓ Apple Brandy
  Shake well and strain into
  cocktail glass. Squeeze
  orange peel on top

1 dash Grenadine   *Twin Six Cocktail*
4 dashes Orange Juice
white of 1 egg
¼ Sweet Vermouth
¾ Dry Gin
  Shake well and strain into
  medium-size glass

1 dash Absinthe   *Ulanda Cocktail*
⅓ Cointreau
⅔ Dry Gin
  Shake well and strain into
  cocktail glass

juice of ¼ Lemon   *Upstairs Cocktail*
2 oz. Dubonnet
  Use medium-size glass and
  fill with soda-water

2 dashes Grand Marnier   *Up-to-Date Cocktail*
2 dashes Angostura Bitters
½ Sherry
½ Rye Whisky
  Shake well and strain into
  cocktail glass

Cocktails

Utility Cocktail

$\frac{1}{2}$ Sherry
$\frac{1}{4}$ Dry Vermouth
$\frac{1}{4}$ Sweet Vermouth
Stir in ice and serve in
cocktail glass

Valencia Cocktail (No. 1)

4 dashes Orange Bitters
$\frac{1}{3}$ Orange Juice
$\frac{2}{3}$ Apricot Brandy
Shake well and strain into
cocktail glass

Valencia Cocktail (No. 2)

4 dashes Orange Bitters
$\frac{1}{3}$ Orange Juice
$\frac{2}{3}$ Apricot Brandy
Shake well, strain into
medium-size glass and fill
with Champagne

Vanderbilt Cocktail

3 dashes Syrup
2 dashes Angostura Bitters
$\frac{1}{4}$ Cherry Brandy
$\frac{3}{4}$ Brandy
Shake well and strain into
cocktail glass

Van Dusen Cocktail

2 dashes Grand Marnier
$\frac{1}{3}$ Dry Vermouth
$\frac{2}{3}$ Dry Gin
Stir well and strain into
cocktail glass

Cocktails

½ Dry Gin   *Velocity Cocktail*
⅔ Sweet Vermouth
1 slice of orange
  Shake well and strain into
  cocktail glass

2 oz. Sweet or Dry Vermouth   *Vermouth Cocktail*
4 dashes Orange or 1 dash
  Angostura Bitters
  Stir well and strain into
  cocktail glass

2 oz. Dry Vermouth   *Vermouth and Cassis*
1 oz. Crème de Cassis   *Cocktail*
  Use medium-size glass and
  fill with soda-water

2 oz. Dry Vermouth   *Vermouth and Curaçao*
½ oz. Curaçao   *Cocktail*
  Use medium-size glass and
  fill with soda-water

¼ Lemon Juice or Lime Juice   *Victors Special Cocktail*
¼ Cointreau
½ Gin
white of 1 egg
  Shake well in ice and strain
  into medium-size glass

½ Grenadine   *Victory Cocktail*
½ Absinthe
  Shake well, strain into
  medium-size glass and fill
  with soda-water

Cocktails

Vie Rose Cocktail

⅛ Lemon Juice
⅛ Grenadine
⅓ Dry Gin
⅓ Kirsch
Shake well and strain into
cocktail glass

Virgin Cocktail

⅓ Forbidden Fruit Liqueur
⅓ White Crème de Menthe
⅓ Dry Gin
Shake well and strain into
cocktail glass

Virgin Special Cocktail
(6 people)

Take a glassful of red-currant
juice, and a half glass of
gooseberry syrup. In
another vessel bruise a
glassful of fresh raspberries
upon which pour
successively a glass of
Brandy, 2 glasses of Gin,
then the currant juice and
gooseberry syrup, and let
stand for half an hour. Then
add a glass of White Wine,
ice, and shake
Serve with either a
raspberry or a small sprig
of red-currants in each glass

Waldorf Cocktail

¼ Lemon Juice
¼ Dry Gin
½ Swedish Punch
Shake well and strain into
cocktail glass

Cocktails

1 teaspoonful Chartreuse
⅓ Sweet Vermouth
⅓ Dry Gin
⅓ Apple Brandy
Shake well and strain into
cocktail glass

Warday's Cocktail

1 teaspoonful Grenadine
¼ Orange Juice
¼ Lemon Juice
½ Rye Whisky
Shake well and strain into
cocktail glass

Ward Eight Cocktail

⅘ Liqueur glass Chartreuse
⅖ Brandy
Use cocktail glass. 1 piece of
peel in glass to form a
circle. Fill with cracked ice.
Pour the liqueur and
Brandy very carefully so
that they do not mix.
Brandy must be poured in
last

Ward's Cocktail

2 dashes Angostura Bitters
2 dashes Syrup
½ Dry Vermouth
½ Brandy
Shake well and strain into
cocktail glass

Washington Cocktail

Cocktails

Waterbury Cocktail

2 dashes Grenadine
½ teaspoon powdered sugar
juice of ¼ Lemon or ½ Lime
white of 1 egg
2 oz. Brandy
   Shake well and strain into
   cocktail glass

Wax Cocktail

3 dashes Orange Bitters
2 oz. Gin
   Shake well and strain into
   cocktail glass

Webster Cocktail

⅛ Lime Juice
⅛ Apricot Brandy
¼ Dry Vermouth
½ Gin
   Shake well and strain into
   cocktail glass

Wedding Belle Cocktail

⅙ Orange Juice
⅙ Cherry Brandy
⅓ Dry Gin
⅓ Dubonnet
   Shake well and strain into
   cocktail glass

Wedding Bells Cocktail
(Sweet)

½ Rye Whisky
⅓ Orange Curaçao
⅙ Lillet
1 dash Orange Bitters
   Stir well with ice

Wedding Bells Cocktail (Dry)

1/3 Rye Whisky
1/3 Lillet
1/6 Curaçao
1/6 Orange Bitters
Stir well with ice

Weesuer Special Cocktail

4 dashes Absinthe
1/4 Dry Vermouth
1/4 Sweet Vermouth
1/4 Orange Curaçao
1/4 Dry Gin
Shake well and strain into cocktail glass

Welcome Stranger Cocktail

1/6 Grenadine
1/6 Lemon Juice
1/6 Orange Juice
1/6 Brandy
1/6 Gin
1/6 Swedish Punch
Shake well and strain into cocktail glass

Wembley Cocktail (No. 1)

1 dash Apricot Brandy
2 dashes Apple Brandy
1/3 Dry Vermouth
2/3 Dry Gin
Shake well and strain into cocktail glass

Cocktails

Wembley Cocktail (No. 2)
⅓ Scotch Whisky
⅓ Dry Vermouth
⅓ Pineapple Juice
Shake well and strain into
cocktail glass

Westbrook Cocktail
(6 people)
3½ glasses Gin
1½ glasses Sweet Vermouth
1 glass Whisky
Before shaking, add a little
castor sugar

Western Rose Cocktail
1 dash Lemon Juice
¼ Dry Vermouth
¼ Apricot Brandy
½ Dry Gin
Shake well and strain into
cocktail glass

West Indian Cocktail
1 teaspoonful sugar in
medium-size tumbler
4 dashes Angostura Bitters
1 teaspoonful Lemon Juice
1 glass Gin
1 lump of ice
Stir and serve in same glass

Which Way Cocktail
⅓ Absinthe
⅓ Anisette
⅓ Brandy
Shake well and strain into
cocktail glass

Cocktails

1 dash Absinthe
3 dashes Curaçao
¼ Dry Vermouth
¼ Sweet Vermouth
½ Brandy
Shake well and strain into
cocktail glass

Whip Cocktail

1 dash Angostura Bitters
4 dashes Syrup
2 oz. Rye Whisky
Stir well and strain into
cocktail glass. Add a cherry

Whisky Cocktail

⅓ Ginger Wine
⅔ Scotch Whisky
Serve in a cocktail glass

Whisky Mac Cocktail

6 oz. Whisky
4 oz. Dry Vermouth
2 oz. Orange Juice
Pour into the shaker and
shake, adding a little nutmeg.
Serve with an olive. This is
a very dry cocktail

Whisky Special Cocktail
(6 people)

Whisky
Dry Vermouth
Sweet Vermouth
Pour into a shaker with
cracked ice. Shake well and
serve

Whisper Cocktail

163

Cocktails

Whist Cocktail

¼ Bacardi Rum
¼ Sweet Vermouth
½ Apple Brandy
Shake well and strain into
cocktail glass

White Cocktail

2 dashes Orange Bitters
2 teaspoonsful Anisette
2 oz. Dry Gin
Stir well and strain into
cocktail glass. Squeeze
lemon peel on top

White Baby Cocktail

½ Gin
¼ Cointreau
¼ Sirop-de-Citron
Shake well and strain into
cocktail glass

White Cargo Cocktail

½ Vanilla Ice Cream
½ Gin
No ice is necessary; just
shake until thoroughly
mixed and add water or
White Wine if the
concoction is too thick

Cocktails

White Lady Cocktail

Lemon Juice
Cointreau
Dry Gin
Shake well and strain into
cocktail glass

Cocktails

White Lily Cocktail

⅓ Cointreau
⅓ Bacardi Rum
⅓ Gin
1 dash Absinthe
Shake well and strain into cocktail glass

White Plush Cocktail

2 oz. Dry Gin
1 oz. Maraschino
½ pint milk
Shake well and strain into long tumbler

White Rose Cocktail

juice of ½ Orange
juice of ¼ Lemon or ½ Lime
white of 1 egg
¼ Maraschino
¾ Dry Gin
Shake well and strain into medium-size glass

White Slave Cocktail

⅓ Champagne
⅓ Gin
⅓ Sherry
white of 1 egg
Shake well in ice and strain into medium-size glass

White Spider Cocktail

½ Vodka
½ Crème de Menthe
Shake well and strain into cocktail glass

Cocktails

⅓ White Crème de Menthe   *White Wings Cocktail*
⅔ Dry Gin
  Shake well and strain into
  cocktail glass

2 dashes Absinthe   *Whizz-Bang Cocktail*
2 dashes Grenadine
2 dashes Orange Bitters
⅓ Dry Vermouth
⅔ Scotch Whisky
  Shake well and strain into
  cocktail glass

⅓ Absinthe   *Whoopee Cocktail*
⅓ Applejack
⅓ Brandy
  Stir well in ice and strain
  into cocktail glass

1 egg   *Widow's Dream Cocktail*
1 oz. Bénédictine
  Shake well, strain into
  medium-size glass and fill up
  with cream

1 dash Angostura Bitters   *Widow's Kiss Cocktail*
¼ Chartreuse
¼ Bénédictine
½ Apple Brandy
  Shake well and strain into
  cocktail glass

Cocktails

Willie Smith Cocktail

1 dash Lemon Juice
⅓ Maraschino
⅔ Brandy
Shake well and strain into cocktail glass

Will Rogers Cocktail

¼ Orange Juice
¼ Dry Vermouth
½ Gin
4 dashes Curaçao
Shake well and strain into cocktail glass

Windy Corner Cocktail

1 glass Blackberry Brandy
Shake well and strain into cocktail glass. Sprinkle a little nutmeg on top

Windsor Rose Cocktail

½ Gin
⅓ Dubonnet
⅙ Campari
1 dash Crème de Noyaux
Stir well and strain into cocktail glass

Woodstock Cocktail

⅔ Applejack
⅓ Dry Vermouth
Stir in ice and strain into cocktail glass

Cocktails

juice of ¼ Orange
½ teaspoonful powdered
  sugar
½ Dry Vermouth
½ Sweet Vermouth
  Shake well and strain into
  medium-size glass and fill
  with soda-water

Wyoming Swing Cocktail

⅓ Cherry Brandy
⅓ Yellow Chartreuse
⅓ Dry Gin
  Shake well and strain into
  cocktail glass

Xanthia Cocktail

1 dash Orange Bitters
1 dash Peach Bitters
2 oz. Sherry
  Stir well and strain into
  cocktail glass

Xeres Cocktail

¼ Lemon Juice
¼ Cointreau
½ Bacardi Rum
  Shake well and strain into
  cocktail glass

X.Y.Z. Cocktail

3 dashes Orange Bitters
1 dash Angostura Bitters
2 oz. Dry Gin
  Shake well and strain into
  small glass. Add a little
  syphon soda and squeeze
  lemon peel on top

Yale Cocktail

Cocktails

Yankee Prince Cocktail

juice of $\frac{1}{4}$ Orange
$\frac{1}{4}$ Grand Marnier
$\frac{3}{4}$ Dry Gin
Shake well and strain into
cocktail glass

Yellow Daisy Cocktail
(6 people)

4 oz. Gin
4 oz. Dry Vermouth
2 oz. Grand Marnier
Before shaking add a dash
of Absinthe

Yellow Parrot Cocktail

$\frac{1}{3}$ Absinthe
$\frac{1}{3}$ Yellow Chartreuse
$\frac{1}{3}$ Apricot Brandy
Shake well and strain into
cocktail glass

Yellow Rattler Cocktail

$\frac{1}{4}$ Orange Juice
$\frac{1}{4}$ Dry Vermouth
$\frac{1}{4}$ Sweet Vermouth
$\frac{1}{4}$ Dry Gin
Shake well and strain into
cocktail glass, with small
crushed pickled onion

Yodel Cocktail

$\frac{1}{2}$ Orange Juice
$\frac{1}{2}$ Fernet Branca
Use medium-size glass and
fill with soda-water

Vodkatini Cocktail

4/5 Vodka
1/5 Dry Vermouth
Stir and strain into cocktail glass. Serve with a twist of lemon peel

Yokohama Cocktail

1 dash Absinthe
1/6 Grenadine
1/6 Vodka
1/3 Orange Juice
1/3 Dry Gin
Shake well and strain into cocktail glass

York Special Cocktail

4 dashes Orange Bitters
1/4 Maraschino
3/4 Dry Vermouth
Shake well and strain into cocktail glass

Young Man Cocktail

1 dash Angostura Bitters
2 dashes Curaçao
1/4 Sweet Vermouth
3/4 Brandy
Shake well and strain into cocktail glass. Add an olive or cherry

Zamba Cocktail

3/4 Rum
1 dash Angostura Bitters
1/4 Lemon Juice
a little Sweet Vermouth
Shake well and strain into cocktail glass. Frost edge of glass

Cocktails

Zanzibar Cocktail
(6 *people*)

juice of 1½ Lemons
2 oz. Gin
6 oz. Dry Vermouth
1 or 2 dessertspoonfuls
  Sugar Syrup
if required, 1 spoonful
  Orange Bitters
  Shake well and serve with
  a piece of lemon rind

Cocktails created since the publication of the last edition

½ Vodka   *Silver Wings*
¼ Cointreau
¼ Dry Vermouth

¼ Dark Rum   *Speedbird*
¼ Dry Vermouth
¼ Sweet Vermouth
¼ Cointreau
  dash of Angostura Bitters
  Twist of Orange

⅓ Cointreau   *Super Savoy*
⅙ Orange Juice
⅙ Campari
  Topped up with Champagne

The 3 cocktails above were
created for British Airways
when Concorde was launched.

2 oz Bacardi Rum   *Shazoom*
2 oz Fresh Orange Juice
1 oz Malibu
  Shake and pour into tall
  tumbler filled with crushed
  ice and top up with
  Lemonade, float dash of
  Pernod

Cocktails

Veranda

2 oz Brandy
1 oz Dry Vermouth
3 oz Orange Juice
Stir in tall tumbler. Add
large twist of Orange Peel

London Pride

$\frac{1}{4}$ oz Gin
$\frac{1}{4}$ oz Passion Juice
$\frac{1}{4}$ oz Amaretto
$\frac{1}{4}$ oz Fresh Cream
Shake and strain into
cocktail glass

Rumfurfe

1 oz Bacardi Rum
$\frac{1}{3}$ oz Passion Juice
$\frac{1}{3}$ oz Fresh Lime Juice
$\frac{1}{3}$ oz Amaretto
dash of Egg White
dash of Gomme Syrup
Shake and top up with soda.
Into tall tumbler filled with
cracked ice add cherry, slice
of orange, slice of lemon

50 Golden Years

$\frac{1}{3}$ oz Passion Juice
$\frac{1}{3}$ oz Apricot Brandy
$\frac{1}{3}$ oz Cointreau
Add dash of Gomme Syrup
Shake and strain into
champagne cocktail glass
and top up with champagne

Cocktails

2 oz Jack Daniels
2 oz Fresh Lemon Juice
  dash of Gomme Syrup
  Stir in tumbler with ice and
  top with ginger beer. Add
  4–5 dashes tobasco sauce

Tobasco Special

$\frac{1}{4}$ oz Gin
$\frac{1}{4}$ oz Orange Juice
$\frac{1}{4}$ oz Lemon Juice
$\frac{1}{4}$ oz Apricot Brandy
  dash of Egg White and
  Gomme Syrup
  Shake and strain into glass
  and add cherry

Sue Barker Special

$\frac{1}{4}$ oz Royal Mint chocolate
$\frac{1}{4}$ oz Amaretto
$\frac{1}{4}$ oz Gin
$\frac{1}{4}$ oz Passion Juice
  Shake and top up with
  Champagne.
  Float strawberry

Windsor Romance
(Created for the
Royal Wedding)

$\frac{1}{3}$ oz Gin
$\frac{1}{3}$ oz Fresh Lime Juice
$\frac{1}{3}$ oz Cherry Heering
  dash Egg White
  dash Gomme Syrup
  Shake and strain into
  cocktail glass (frosted)
  Add cherry

Savoy Valentine

Cocktails

Blue Haze

$\frac{1}{2}$ oz Vodka
$\frac{1}{4}$ oz Cointreau
$\frac{1}{4}$ oz Dry Vermouth
dash Blue Curacao
Stir and strain into
champagne glass filled with
crushed ice. Add cherry,
slice of orange and lemon

Savoy Springtime

$\frac{1}{4}$ oz Gin
$\frac{1}{4}$ oz Cointreau
$\frac{1}{4}$ oz Poire William
$\frac{1}{4}$ oz Orange Juice (shake)
dash Orange Juice
Top with Champagne

Savoy Ideal

1 oz Apricot Brandy
1 oz Pineapple Juice
1 oz Fresh Double Cream
dash of Cointreau and
Gomme Syrup
Shake and strain into
champagne glass
Add slice of lime and 2
cherries on stick

Royal Delight
(Created at the birth of
Prince William)

$\frac{1}{3}$ oz Gin
$\frac{1}{3}$ oz Fresh Lime Juice
$\frac{1}{3}$ oz Fraise de Bordeaux
dash of Egg White and
Gomme Syrup
Shake and strain into glass
with crushed ice. Add
strawberry and whole slice
of lime

Cocktails

$\frac{1}{3}$ oz Gin
$\frac{1}{3}$ oz Fresh Lime Juice
$\frac{1}{3}$ oz Blue Curacao
dash of Egg White and
Gomme Syrup
Strain into cocktail glass

Cambridge

$\frac{1}{3}$ oz Gin
$\frac{1}{6}$ oz Dry Vermouth
$\frac{1}{6}$ oz Triple Sec
4 dashes Blue Vegetable
Extract
Stir and strain

Oxford

$\frac{1}{3}$ oz Cointreau
$\frac{1}{3}$ oz Fraise de Bordeaux
2 whole Strawberries
3 oz White Wine
Blend in blender with little
ice

Dawn Sunrise
(lighter cocktail)

$\frac{1}{2}$ oz Tequila
$\frac{1}{4}$ oz Medori
$\frac{1}{4}$ oz Malibu
Stir and strain

Something Special

$\frac{1}{4}$ oz Dark Rum
$\frac{1}{8}$ oz Campari
$\frac{1}{8}$ oz Sweet Vermouth
$\frac{1}{8}$ oz Fresh Lime Juice
$\frac{1}{8}$ oz Cherry Heering
dash of Grenadine
Shake and strain

The Bodysnatcher
(Created for
Mme Tussaud's
Chamber of Horrors)

Cocktails

Tip of the Tongue

$\frac{1}{3}$ oz Medori
$\frac{1}{3}$ oz Passion Juice
$\frac{1}{3}$ oz Gin
dash of Egg White and
Syrup
Shake and strain
Top up with Champagne

Wimbledon '84

$\frac{1}{2}$ oz Fraise de Bordeaux
$\frac{1}{4}$ oz Amaretto
$\frac{1}{4}$ oz Fresh Lemon Juice
2 Strawberries
$\frac{1}{4}$ oz Cream
Blend in shaker and garnish
with strawberry

Fraise Royale

2 Strawberries (crushed)
Topped up with Champagne

Pêche Royale

$\frac{1}{2}$ Crushed Peach
Topped up with Champagne

Savoy Royale

$\frac{1}{2}$ Peach (crushed)
2 Strawberries (crushed)
Topped up with Champagne

Savoy 90

$\frac{3}{4}$ oz Amaretto
$\frac{1}{4}$ oz Fresh Lime Juice
Topped up with Champagne

Royal Silver
(Silver Jubilee)

$\frac{1}{2}$ oz Cointreau
$\frac{1}{2}$ oz Poire William
1 oz Grapefruit Juice
Topped up with Champagne

Cocktails

$\frac{1}{4}$ oz Fresh Lime Juice
$\frac{1}{4}$ oz Passion Juice
$\frac{1}{4}$ oz Fraise de Bordeaux
$\frac{1}{4}$ oz Peach Liquor
dash of Egg White
Shaken and topped up with
Champagne

Savoy Affair

$\frac{1}{2}$ oz Vodka
$\frac{1}{4}$ oz Framboise
$\frac{3}{4}$ oz Fresh Lime Juice
1 dash Gomme Syrup
1 dash Blue Curacao
Shaken

Maggie Blue
(Margaret Thatcher)

1 oz Passion Fruit Juice
$\frac{1}{2}$ oz Cherry Heering
$\frac{1}{2}$ oz Brandy
Shaken and topped up with
Champagne

Lady of Mey
(Queen Mother's
80th Birthday)

oz Vodka
oz Fresh Grapefruit Juice
oz Poire William
oz Crème de Noyau
Shaken
Rim balloon glass with
sugar

Silver Balloons
(to celebrate the
first balloon crossing
of the Atlantic)

oz gin
oz Fresh Orange Juice
oz Framboise
oz Galliano
Shaken and topped up with
Champagne

Covent Garden Cocktail
(to celebrate opening of
new market)

179

Cocktails

Down Your Way Cocktail

$\frac{1}{3}$ oz Gin
$\frac{1}{3}$ oz Cinzano rose
$\frac{1}{3}$ oz Fresh Orange Juice
Shaken. Strain into cocktail
glass and add cherry

Moonwalk

1 oz Grand Marnier
1 oz Grapefruit Juice
2 dashes of Orange Flower
Water
Shake and pour into
champagne glass.
Top with Champagne

High Life

$\frac{1}{2}$ oz Brandy
$\frac{1}{4}$ oz Cordial Medoc
$\frac{1}{8}$ oz Apricot Brandy
$\frac{1}{8}$ oz Fresh Lime Juice

The Hook

$\frac{1}{6}$ oz Cherry Brandy
$\frac{1}{6}$ oz Apricot Brandy
$\frac{1}{3}$ oz Passion Fruit
$\frac{1}{2}$ oz Vodka

Jane's Pick You Up

$\frac{1}{4}$ oz Fresh Orange Juice
$\frac{1}{8}$ oz Ricard
$\frac{1}{8}$ oz Dry Vermouth
$\frac{1}{2}$ oz Vodka
3 dashes of Fernet Branca

Cocktails

¼ oz Brandy	*Nancy*
¼ oz Benedictine	(after dinner drink)
½ oz White Port	
Add large twist of orange peel. Put into an old fashioned glass filled with ice	

⅓ oz Curacao	*Outlook 10*
⅓ oz Framboise	
⅓ oz Fresh Orange Juice	
Shake and strain into champagne glass	
Top with Champagne	

½ oz Bourbon	*76*
¼ oz Yellow Chartreuse	
¼ oz Fresh Lime Juice	
2 dashes Egg White	
Shake well and strain into a cocktail glass. Add cherry	

oz Gin	*Happy Return*
oz Lemon Juice	
oz Cherry Brandy	
oz Cointreau	

oz Cherry Brandy	*Prince of Wales*
oz Lemon Juice	
Blended with a strawberry	
Topped up with Champagne	

Prepared Cocktails
for bottling

5 gallons Gin
2 gallons water
1 quart Gomme Syrup
2 oz. Tincture of Orange Peel
2 oz. Tincture of Gentian
½ oz. Tincture of Cardamoms
½ oz. Tincture of Lemon Peel
  Mix together and give the
  desired colour with
  Solferino and caramel, in
  equal proportions

Gin Cocktail

5 gallons Bourbon Rye
2 gallons water
1 quart Gomme Syrup
2 oz. Tincture of Orange Peel
1 oz. Tincture of Lemon Peel
1 oz. Tincture of Gentian
½ oz. Tincture of Cardamoms
  Mix these ingredients
  thoroughly and colour with
  Solferino and caramel, in
  equal proportions

Bourbon Cocktail

5 gallons Strong Brandy
2 gallons water
1 quart Bitters
1 quart Gomme Syrup
1 bottle Curaçao
  Mix thoroughly and filter
  through Canton Flannel

Brandy Cocktail

Prepared Cocktails for Bottling

Brandy Cocktail
(*Another recipe*)

5 gallons Brandy
2 gallons water
1 quart Gomme Syrup
¼ pint Essence of Cognac
1 oz. Tincture of Cloves
1 oz. Tincture of Gentian
2 oz. Tincture of Orange Peel
¼ oz. Tincture of Cardamoms
½ oz. Tincture of Liquorice Root
Mix the essence and tinctures with a portion of the spirits; add the remainder of the ingredients and colour with a sufficient quantity of Solferino and caramel (in equal proportions) to give the desired colour

Non-Alcoholic Cocktails

⅓ Lemon Juice   *Cinderella Cocktail*
⅓ Orange Juice
⅓ Pineapple Juice
  Shake and strain into
  cocktail glass

1 egg   *Egg Nogg Cocktail*
1 teaspoon soft sugar
½ pint of milk
  Shake and strain into a tall
  glass. Grate nutmeg on top

Put into tumbler   *First Aid Cocktail*
  juice of 1 Lime
1 teaspoon sugar
1 tablespoon Blackcurrant
  Syrup
  cracked ice
  Fill with soda or plain
  water
  Decorate with slice of Lime

⅛ Grenadine   *Keep Sober Cocktail*
⅛ Sirop-de-Citron
¾ Tonic
  Serve in long glass and fill
  with syphon soda

Non-Alcoholic Cocktails

Long Boat Cocktail

Use long tumbler
2 oz. Lime Juice Cordial
2 lumps ice
Fill with Ginger Beer
Decorate with sprigs of
fresh mint

Parson's Special Cocktail

4 dashes Grenadine
2 oz. Orange Juice
yolk of 1 egg
Shake well and strain into
medium-size glass

Parson's Walk Cocktail

Put into long tumbler
juice of 1 Orange
1 lump of ice
Fill with Ginger Ale
Decorate with slice of
orange

Pussy Foot Cocktail

⅓ Orange Juice
⅓ Lemon Juice
⅓ Lime Juice
dash of Grenadine
yolk of one egg
Shake and strain into
medium-size glass
Add cherry and slice of
orange
Splash of soda

Non-Alcoholic Cocktails

Put into tumbler
  juice of 1 Lemon
1½ teaspoonsful sugar
1 tablespoon Raspberry Syrup
  cracked ice
  Fill with soda or plain water
  Decorate with slice of lemon

Raspberry Lemonade Cocktail

Use long tumbler
  Juice of 1 Lemon
1 oz of Lime Juice Cordial
½ teaspoon Grenadine
2 lumps of ice
  Fill with tonic water
  Decorate with slice of lemon

Sportsman Cocktail

3 oz Tomato Juice
2 dashes Worcester Sauce
2 pinches celery salt
  Shake and strain into
  cocktail glass

Tomato Cocktail

Put into cocktail shaker
½ Lemon Juice
½ Pineapple Juice
1 teaspoon Grenadine
  white of 1 egg
  Shake well
  Pour into long stem glass
  add 1 lump of ice
  Fill with lemonade
  Decorate with cherry and
  slice of orange

Tonga Cocktail

Sours

A Sour is usually prepared from the following recipe

juice of ½ Lemon
1 teaspoonful sugar
2 oz. of spirit or liqueur
Shake well and strain into medium-size glass. Add one
squirt of soda-water, 1 slice of orange and a cherry

Egg Sour

1 teaspoon powdered white
sugar
2 dashes Lemon Juice
1 oz. Curaçao
1 oz. Brandy
1 egg
2 or 3 small lumps of ice
Shake well and remove ice
before serving

Toddies

baked apple   *Apple Toddy*
oz. Applejack
teaspoonful sugar
Use medium-size stem glass.
Fill with hot water and
serve with a spoon. Grate
nutmeg on top

issolve 1 lump of sugar in a   *Brandy Toddy*
edium-size glass, and add
oz. of Brandy and a lump
f ice

oz. Rum   *Hot Spiced Rum Toddy*
teaspoonful sugar
Add a few cloves and twist
lemon peel on top. If
desired, weaken with a little
water. Use medium-size
stem glass and serve with a
spoon

teaspoonful sugar   *Whisky Toddy*
oz. Whisky
oz. water
Stir and serve

Flips

The Flip, especially the kind made with Rum, is famous as a sailor's drink. It is usually made in the following way:

Rum Flip

1 egg
½ tablespoonful powdered
   sugar
2 oz. Rum, Brandy, Port
   Wine, Sherry or Whisky
   Shake well and strain into
   medium-size glass. Grate a
   little nutmeg on top. In
   cold weather a dash of
   ginger can be added

Ale Flip

Put 1 quart of Ale in a
saucepan and bring slowly
to boil. Beat up the whites
of 2 eggs and the yolks of
4 separately. Add them
gradually to 4 tablespoonfuls
of moist sugar, and a half
of nutmeg grated. When all
are well mixed together
pour on the boiling Ale
slowly, meanwhile beating
the mixture constantly. The
mixture should then be
poured rapidly from one
jug being held well above
the other in order to ensure
a fine, smooth froth. This
is an excellent remedy to
take when you suspect the
beginning of a cold

Egg Noggs

Egg Nogg

egg
tablespoonful powdered
sugar
oz. of any spirit desired
ll glass with milk
Shake well and strain into
long tumbler. Grate a little
nutmeg on top

Baltimore Egg Nogg

fresh egg
tablespoonful sugar
oz. Brandy
oz. Rum
oz. Madeira
pint fresh milk
Shake well and strain into
long tumbler. Grate nutmeg
on top

Breakfast Egg Nogg

fresh egg
Curaçao
Brandy
pint fresh milk
Shake well and strain into
long tumbler. Grate nutmeg
on top

*General Harrison's
Egg Nogg*

egg
teaspoonfuls sugar
or 3 small lumps of ice.
Fill the tumbler with Cider
and shake well

Egg Noggs

Punch Style Egg Nogg
(6 people)

Beat up 12 eggs into a punch-bowl and add a tablespoonful of powdered sugar to each egg. Add 1 quart of Sherry or any other spirit, and 4 pints of hot or cold milk. Sprinkle nutmeg on top, stir well, and serve in stem glasses with a spoon

Coolers

Juice of ½ Lemon or 1 Lime
dashes Grenadine
oz. Apricot Brandy
Shake well, strain into long
tumbler and fill with soda-
water

Apricot Cooler

oz. Dry Vermouth
teaspoonful Grenadine
lumps of ice
Pour into tumbler and fill
up with soda-water

Country Club Cooler

oz. Bacardi Rum
Juice of ½ fresh Lime
Use long tumbler. Add ice
and lime rind, and fill up
with Coca-Cola

Cuba Libre Cooler

Juice of ½ Lemon or 1 Lime
tablespoonful sugar
oz. Applejack
Shake well, strain into long
tumbler and fill with soda-
water

Harvard Cooler

teaspoonful powdered
sugar
Juice of ½ Lemon
dashes Angostura Bitters
oz. Scotch Whisky
lump of ice
Use long tumbler and fill
with Ginger Ale

Highland Cooler

Coolers

Lone Tree Cooler

juice of ¼ Lemon
juice of 1 Orange
⅓ Dry Vermouth
⅔ Dry Gin
1 oz. Grenadine
Shake well, strain into
tumbler and fill with soda-
water

Lone Reign Cooler

1 dash Angostura Bitters
2 oz. Rye Whisky
¼ measure Marnique
juice of ½ Orange
juice of ½ Lemon
Top up with Ginger Ale
in a long tumbler

Manhattan Cooler

juice of ½ Lemon or 1 Lime
½ tablespoonful powdered
sugar
2 oz. Claret
3 dashes Rum
Stir well and strain into
medium-size glass. Decora
with fruit in season

Mint Cooler

2 oz. Scotch Whisky
3 dashes Crème de Menthe
Use a tumbler; add a lump
of ice and fill with soda-
water

Coolers

Moonlight Cooler

tablespoonful powdered
 sugar
uice of 1 Lemon
 oz. Apple Brandy
 Shake well and strain into
 long tumbler. Fill with
 soda-water and decorate
 with slices of fruit in season

Moscow Mule Cooler

 oz. Vodka
 dash Lime Juice
 Add 2 lumps of ice, serve
 in long tumbler and fill
 with Ginger Beer. Decorate
 with a slice of lime and a
 sprig of fresh mint

Planter's Punch Cooler

 oz. Lemon or Lime Juice
 oz. Gomme Syrup
 dash Angostura Bitters
 oz. Jamaica Rum
 Shake; pour unstrained into
 tall tumbler, add a slice of
 pineapple and a slice of
 orange, and serve with
 straws

Remsen Cooler

 oz. Dry Gin
 split of Soda
 Peel rind of lemon in spiral
 form, place in long
 tumbler with a lump of ice,
 add Gin and fill with soda-
 water

Coolers

Sea Breeze Cooler

juice of ½ Lemon
2 dashes Grenadine
½ Apricot Brandy
½ Dry Gin
1 lump of ice
   Use long tumbler and fill
   with soda-water. 2 sprigs of
   fresh mint on top

Shady Grove Cooler

½ tablespoonful sugar
juice of ½ Lemon
2 oz. Dry Gin
   Use long tumbler and fill
   with Ginger Beer

Tom Collins

Juice of ½ Lemon
½ tablespoonful powdered
   sugar
2 oz. Dry Gin
   Shake well and strain into
   long tumbler. Add a lump
   of ice and a split of soda-
   water

Tom Collins

5 or 6 dashes Gomme Syrup
Juice of 1 small Lemon
2 oz. Whisky
2 or 3 lumps of ice
   Shake well and strain into
   long tumbler. Add a lump
   of ice and a split of soda-
   water

Whisky Collins

Juice of ½ Lemon
tablespoonful powdered
   sugar
oz. Hollands Gin
   Shake well and strain into
   long tumbler. Add a lump
   of ice and a split of soda-
   water

John Collins

Slings

dissolve 1 teaspoonful of
sugar in water
2 oz. Dry Gin
1 lump of ice
Serve in long tumbler and
fill with water or soda-water.
If served hot, grate a little
nutmeg on top

Gin Sling

juice of ¼ Lemon
¼ Dry Gin
½ Cherry Brandy
Shake well, strain into
medium-size glass and fill
with soda. Add a
lump of ice

Singapore Sling

Place in a shaker 8 oz. of Gin,
2 oz. of Bénédictine, 2 oz. of
Cherry Brandy, the juice of
2 lemons, 1 teaspoonful of
Angostura Bitters, and one
of Orange Bitters
Shake sufficiently and serve
in large glasses, filling up
with soda-water

Straits Sling
(6 people)

Sangarees

1 teaspoonful powdered
  sugar
2 oz. Sherry or Port
  Stir well and strain into
  medium-size glass, add a
  slice of orange or lemon
  peel and grate a little
  nutmeg on top

Savoy Sangaree

2 oz. Sherry
1 teaspoon fine sugar
  Fill tumbler ⅓ full with ice
  and grate nutmeg on top

Sherry Sangaree

1⅓ wineglasses Port Wine
1 teaspoonful sugar
  Fill tumbler ⅔ full with ice.
  Shake well and grate
  nutmeg on top

Port Wine Sangaree

Shrubs

To the thin rinds of 2 lemons
and the juice of 5, add 2
quarts of Brandy; cover for
3 days, then add a quart of
of Sherry and 2 lb. of loaf
sugar, run it through a
jelly bag and bottle it

Brandy Shrub

1 pint sugar
1 pint strained Currant Juice
    Boil it gently for 8 or 10
    minutes, skimming it well;
    take it off and, when
    lukewarm, add half a gill of
    Brandy to every pint of
    Shrub. Bottle tight

Currant Shrub

Put 3 pints of Orange Juice
and 1 lb. of loaf sugar
to a gallon of Rum. Put all
into a cask, and leave it for
6 weeks when it will be
ready for use

Rum Shrub

Strip the fruit, and prepare in
a jar, as for jelly; strain the
juice, of which put 2
quarts to 1 gallon of Rum,
and 2 lb. of lump sugar.
    Strain through a jelly bag.

White Currant Shrub

Highballs

Highballs are usually prepared from this basic recipe:

1 lump of ice
2 oz. spirit, liqueur or wine
    Use long tumbler and fill with soda-water or Ginger Ale.
    Add a twist of lemon peel

1 oz. Amer Picon   *Amer Picon Highball*
3 dashes Grenadine
1 lump of ice
    Fill long tumbler with soda-
    water or Ginger Ale. Add a
    twist of lemon peel

1½ oz. Brandy   *Horse's Neck Highball*
2 dashes Angostura Bitters
2 lumps of ice
    Use long tumbler and fill
    with Ginger Ale. Peel the
    rind of a lemon spirally in
    one piece and place one end
    over the edge of the
    tumbler, allowing the
    remainder to curl inside

1 lump of ice   *Perry or Champagne*
2 oz. Scotch Whisky   *Cider Highball*
    Use a goblet and fill with
    Cider or Perry

Fizzes

juice of ½ Lemon
½ tablespoonful powdered
    sugar
2 oz. Dry Gin
    Shake well, strain into
    medium-size glass and fill
    with soda-water. Add 2
    sprigs of fresh mint

Alabama Fizz

juice of ½ Lemon
½ tablespoonful powdered
    sugar
2 oz. Gin
    Shake well, strain into
    medium-size glass and fill
    with soda-water. Add a
    teaspoonful of Raspberry
    Syrup

Albemarle Fizz

white of 1 egg
4 dashes Lemon Juice
1 teaspoonful powdered sugar
2 oz. Apple Brandy
    Shake well, strain into
    medium-size glass and fill
    with soda-water

Apple Blow Fizz

juice of ½ Lemon
½ tablespoonful powdered
    sugar
2 oz. Brandy
    Shake well, strain into
    medium-size glass and fill
    with syphon soda-water

Brandy Fizz

Fizzes

Bucks Fizz

½ oz. Orange Juice
Use a wineglass and fill
with Champagne

Cream Fizz

juice of ½ Lemon
½ tablespoonful powdered
sugar
2 oz. Dry Gin
1 teaspoonful fresh cream
Shake well, strain into
medium-size glass and fill
with soda-water

Derby Fizz

5 dashes Lemon Juice
1 teaspoonful powdered
sugar
1 egg
2 oz. Rye or Scotch Whisky
3 dashes Curaçao
Shake well, strain into
medium-size glass and fill
with soda-water

Dubonnet Fizz

juice of ½ Orange
juice of ¼ Lemon
1 teaspoonful Cherry Brandy
2 oz. Dubonnet
Shake well, strain into
medium-size glass and fill
with soda-water

Fizzes

Gin Fizz

Juice of ½ Lemon
½ tablespoonful powdered
  sugar
2 oz. Gin
  Shake well, strain into
  medium-size glass and fill
  with syphon soda-water

Golden Fizz

Juice of ½ Lemon
½ tablespoonful powdered
  sugar
2 oz. Gin
Yolk of 1 egg
  Shake well, strain into
  medium-size glass and fill
  with syphon soda-water

Grand Royal Fizz

Juice of ½ Lemon
½ tablespoonful powdered
  sugar
2 oz. Gin
2 dashes Maraschino
Juice of ¼ Orange
1 tablespoonful sweet cream
  Shake well, strain into
  medium-size glass and fill
  with syphon soda-water

Fizzes

Hoffmann Fizz

juice of ½ Lemon
½ tablespoonful powdered
   sugar
2 oz. Gin
   Shake well, strain into
   medium-size glass and fill
   with syphon soda-water.
   Add teaspoonful of
   Grenadine

Holland Fizz

juice of ½ Lemon
½ tablespoonful powdered
   sugar
2 oz. Gin
white of 1 egg
   Shake well, strain into
   medium-size glass and fill
   with syphon soda-water.
   Add 3 sprigs of fresh mint

Imperial Fizz

juice of ½ Lemon
⅓ Rum
⅔ Rye or Scotch Whisky
½ tablespoonful sugar
   Shake well, strain into
   medium-size glass and fill
   with syphon soda-water

May Blossom Fizz

1 teaspoonful Grenadine
juice of ½ Lemon
1 oz. Swedish Punch
   Shake well, strain into
   medium-size glass and fill
   with soda-water

Fizzes

Morning Glory Fizz

juice of ½ Lemon or 1 Lime
½ tablespoonful powdered
    sugar
white of 1 egg
2 dashes Absinthe
2 oz. Scotch Whisky
    Shake well, strain into long
    tumbler and fill with syphon
    soda-water

New Orleans Gin Fizz

juice of ½ Lemon
½ tablespoonful powdered
    sugar
white of 1 egg
2 oz. Dry Gin
2 dashes Orange-flower
1 tablespoonful sweet cream
    Shake well, strain into long
    tumbler and fill with syphon
    soda-water

Ohio Fizz

½ Lemon Juice
½ Orange Juice
    Use medium-size glass and
    fill with Champagne

Orange Fizz

juice of ½ Orange
juice of ¼ Lemon or ½ Lime
2 oz. Dry Gin
    Shake well, strain into
    medium-size glass and fill
    with syphon soda-water

Fizzes

Orgeat Fizz

juice of ½ Lemon
1 oz. Orgeat
  Shake well, strain into
  medium-size glass and fill
  with soda-water

Ostend Fizz

½ oz. Crème de Cassis
½ oz. Kirsch
  Shake well, strain into
  medium-size glass and fill
  with soda-water

Peach Blow Fizz

juice of ½ Lemon or 1 Lime
4 mashed Strawberries
½ tablespoonful powdered
  sugar
1 tablespoonful sweet cream
2 oz. Dry Gin
  Shake well, strain into
  medium-size glass and fill
  with syphon soda-water

Pineapple Fizz

2 tablespoonfuls Pineapple
  Juice
½ tablespoonful powdered
  sugar
2 oz. Bacardi Rum
  Shake well, strain into
  medium-size glass and fill
  with syphon soda-water

Fizzes

<table>
<tr><td>

juice of ½ Lemon
½ tablespoonful powdered
  sugar
2 oz. Gin
1 egg
  Shake well, strain into
  medium-size glass and fill
  with syphon soda-water

</td><td>

Royal Fizz

</td></tr>
</table>

juice of ½ Lemon
½ tablespoonful powdered
  sugar
white of 1 egg
2 dashes Raspberry or
  Grenadine Syrup
2 oz. Sloe Gin
  Shake well, strain into
  medium-size glass and fill
  with syphon soda-water

Ruby Fizz

juice of ½ Lemon
½ tablespoonful powdered
  sugar
2 oz. Gin
white of 1 egg
  Shake well, strain into
  medium-size glass and fill
  with syphon soda-water

Silver Fizz

Fizzes

South Side Fizz

juice of ½ Lemon
½ tablespoonful powdered
  sugar
2 oz. Gin
  Shake well, strain into
  medium-size glass and fill
  with syphon soda-water.
  Add fresh mint leaves

Texas Fizz

juice of ¼ Orange and ¼
  Lemon
1 teaspoonful powdered
  sugar
2 oz. Dry Gin
  Shake well, strain into
  medium-size glass and fill
  with syphon soda-water

Rickeys

Most Rickeys are made with this recipe:

1 lump of ice
juice of ½ Lime or ¼ Lemon
2 oz. of any spirit or liqueur fancied—Whisky, Gin, Rum,
　　Bourbon, Apple Brandy, Caperitif, etc.
　　Use medium-size glass. Fill with Carbonated Water and
　　leave rind of lime or lemon in glass.

1 lump of ice　　　　　　　　　　　　*Savoy Rickey*
juice of ½ Lime or ¼ Lemon
2 oz. Gin
4 dashes Grenadine
　　Fill with Carbonated Water
　　and leave rind of lime or
　　Lemon in glass. Use
　　medium-size glass

Daisies

juice of ½ Lemon   *Gin Daisy*
¼ tablespoonful powdered
   sugar
6 dashes Grenadine
2 oz. Gin
   Use long tumbler. Half fill
   with cracked ice and stir
   until glass is frosted. Fill
   with syphon soda-water,
   put 4 sprigs of green mint
   on top and decorate with
   slices of fruit in season

3 or 4 dashes Gomme Syrup   *Santa Cruz Rum Daisy*
2 or 3 dashes Maraschino or
   Curaçao
juice of ½ small Lemon
2 oz. Rum
   Fill glass ⅓ full with shaved
   ice. Shake thoroughly,
   strain into a small tumbler
   and fill up with Seltzer
   Water

3 dashes Gomme Syrup   *Whisky Daisy*
juice of ½ small Lemon
2 oz. Bourbon or Rye Whisky
   Fill glass ⅓ full with shaved
   ice. Shake thoroughly,
   strain into small tumbler
   and fill up with Seltzer
   Water

Fixes

In making fixes be careful to put the lemon rind in the glass.

Place in a small tumbler   *Brandy Fix*
teaspoonful of sugar,
teaspoonful of water to
dissolve the sugar, juice of
Lemon, ½ oz. of Cherry
Brandy and 1 oz. of Brandy
Fill the glass with fine ice
and stir slowly; add a slice
of lemon and serve with a
straw

tablespoonful sugar   *Gin Fix*
Lemon
oz. water
oz. Gin
Fill ⅔ full with shaved ice.
Stir with a spoon and
decorate with fruit in
season

The Santa Cruz Fix is made   *Santa Cruz Fix*
by substituting Rum for
Brandy in the Brandy Fix

Fixes

Whisky Fix

1 large teaspoonful of
powdered white sugar,
dissolved in a little water
juice of ½ Lemon
2 oz. Bourbon or Rye
Whisky
Use small tumbler. Fill
about ⅔ full with shaved ice
stir well, and decorate on
top with fruit in season

Juleps

The Julep is a drink that originated in the Southern States of America. It was Captain Marryat of the Royal Navy and famous novelist who introduced the beverage into the British Isles, and below we quote his recipe in his own words:

"I must descant a little upon the mint julep, as it is, with the thermometer at 100 degrees, one of the most delightful and insinuating potations that ever was invented, and may be drunk with equal satisfaction when the thermometer is as low as 70 degrees. There are many varieties such as those composed of Claret, Madeira, etc., but the ingredients of the real mint julep are as follows. I learned how to make them, and succeeded pretty well. Put into a tumbler about a dozen sprigs of the tender shoots of mint, upon them put a spoonful of white sugar, and equal proportions of Peach and common Brandy, so as to fill it up one-third, or perhaps a little less. Then take rasped or pounded ice, and fill up the tumbler. Epicures rub the lips of the tumbler with a piece of fresh pineapple, and the tumbler itself is very often incrusted outside with stalactites of ice. As the ice melts, you drink. I once overheard two ladies talking in the next room to me, and one of them said, 'Well, if I have a weakness for any one thing, it is for a mint julep!'—a very amiable weakness, and proving her good sense and good taste. They are, in fact, like the American ladies, irresistible."

Juleps

Champagne Julep

Use long tumbler
1 lump of sugar
2 sprigs mint
    Fill glass with Champagne.
    Stir gently and decorate
    with slices of fruit in season

Perry or Champagne Cider Julep

Use tumbler
1 lump of sugar
2 sprigs mint
    Fill glass with Cider or
    Perry. Stir gently and
    decorate with slices of fruit
    in season

Pineapple Julep
(6 people)

Take a large glass jug and fill
it ¼ full with crushed ice.
Pour in the juice of 2
oranges, 2 oz. of Raspberry
Vinegar, 2 oz. of
Maraschino, 3 oz. of Gin,
and a bottle of Sparkling
Moselle or Saumur. Pull a
pineapple to pieces with a
silver fork and place the
pieces in the jug. Stir the
mixture, add a little fruit
for appearance's sake, and
serve

Juleps

Southern Mint Julep

4 sprigs fresh mint
½ tablespoonful powdered
  sugar
2 oz. Bourbon or Rye Whisky
  Use long tumbler and crush
  the mint leaves and
  dissolved sugar lightly
  together, add spirits and fill
  glass with cracked ice; stir
  gently until glass is frosted.
  Decorate on top with 3
  sprigs of mint

Smashes

A Smash is a kind of junior Julep usually prepared from
this basic recipe:

Dissolve 1 lump of sugar in a medium-size glass and add
  leaves of mint, crushing the sugar and mint lightly together.
Put a lump of ice in the glass and then add 2 oz. of
Bacardi Rum, Brandy, Gin or Whisky.
Decorate with a slice of orange and squeeze lemon peel on top

Cobblers

The Cobbler, like the Julep, originated as a drink in America. Although it is now a universal favourite it is primarily a drink for hot climates. It is delightfully easy to make and should be decorated with whichever fruits are in season.

Fill glass ½ full with cracked ice
Add 1 teaspoonful powdered sugar
Add 2 oz. Gin (or Whisky, or Brandy if preferred)
Stir well and decorate with slices of orange or pineapple

Frappé

For Frappé all kinds of liqueurs may be used. A 5 oz. stemmed glass is filled with snow ice, and 1 oz. of the desired liqueur is then poured on to the ice. The drink is served with short straws. Frappé may also be prepared with more than one liqueur.

⅔ Absinthe   *Absinthe Frappé*
⅓ Syrup of Anisette
double quantity of water
   Shake up until the outside
   of the shaker is thoroughly
   covered with ice. Strain
   into a small tumbler

Punches

The proper preparation of Punch needs a great deal of care but the one great secret in its concoction is just that the various subtle ingredients must be so mixed that no one taste is more noticeable than another. This depends not so much upon the exact proportions of the different ingredients as upon the order in which they are added to the punch bowl. Here are selections of recipes old and new:

Bombay Punch

quart Brandy
quart Sherry
pint Maraschino
pint Orange Curaçao
quarts Champagne
quarts Carbonated Water
Stir gently and surround
punch bowl with cracked
ice, decorating with fruits
in season

Brandy Punch

ce of 15 lemons
ce of 4 oranges
lb. powdered sugar
pint Curaçao
oz. Grenadine
quarts Brandy
Place a large block of ice in
a punch bowl; add the
above ingredients and from
one to two quarts of
sparkling mineral water

Punches

Cardinal Punch

1½ lb. sugar
2 quarts sparkling mineral water
2 quarts Claret
1 pint Brandy
1 pint Rum
1 pint sparkling white wine
2 oz. Sweet Vermouth
Place in a punch bowl with a large block of ice

Champagne Punch

½ lb. powdered sugar
2 quarts Champagne
1 quart sparkling mineral water
2 oz. Brandy
2 oz. Maraschino
2 oz. Curaçao
Mix well in punch bowl. Surround bowl with cracked ice and add slices of fruit in season

Punches

Claret Punch

lb. powdered sugar
quarts Claret
quarts sparkling mineral
water
pint Lemon Juice
oz. Curaçao
Mix well in punch bowl.
Surround bowl with cracked
ice and add slices of fruit in
season

Fish House Punch

ice of 6 Lemons
lb. powdered sugar
pint Brandy
pint Peach Brandy
pint Jamaica Rum
pints sparkling mineral
water
Use large punch bowl with
block of ice

Punches

Milk Punch (No. 1)

juice of 4 Lemons
rind of 2 Lemons
½ lb. white sugar, dissolved
in just sufficient hot water
1 Pineapple, peeled, sliced
and pounded
6 Cloves
20 Coriander Seeds
1 small stick Cinnamon
1 pint Brandy
1 pint Jamaica Rum
1 gill Batavia Arrack
1 cup strong green tea
1 quart boiling water
1 quart hot milk
Put all the materials in a
clean demijohn, the boiling
water to be added last; cor
this down to prevent
evaporation, and allow the
ingredients to steep for at
least 6 hours; then add the
hot milk and the juice of
2 more lemons; mix and
filter through a jelly bag;
and when the punch has
passed bright, put it away
tightly-corked bottles

This punch is intended to be iced for drinking.
If intended for immediate use, filtering is not necessary.

Punches

Milk Punch (No. 2)

1 glass milk
½ tablespoonful powdered
   sugar
2 oz. Whisky or Rum
   Shake well and strain into
   long tumbler, grating a little
   nutmeg on top

*Perry or Champagne
Cider Punch*

¼ lb. powdered sugar
1 spirit measure Brandy
1 oz. Maraschino
1 oz. Curaçao
   Mix well in punch bowl.
   Surround bowl with
   cracked ice and add slices of
   fruit in season

Planter's Punch
(see *coolers*)

Rhine Wine Punch
(*10 people*)

½ lb. powdered sugar
3 quarts Rhine wine
1 quart sparkling mineral
   water
2 oz. Brandy
1 oz. Maraschino
2 tablespoonfuls tea
   Put the tea in a small piece
   of cheese-cloth and leave in
   the above mixture for about
   10 minutes. Surround punch
   bowl with cracked ice and
   add slices of fruit in season

239

Punches

Roman Punch

1 quart Champagne
1 quart Rum
½ oz. Orange Bitters
juice of 10 Lemons
juice of 3 Oranges
2 lb. sugar
whites of 10 eggs
  Use punch bowl. Dissolve
  sugar in lemon and orange
  juice, add the rind of 1
  orange, add the well-beaten
  whites of eggs. Surround
  the bowl with cracked ice
  and stir the ingredients
  well together

Rum Punch
(25 people)

1 bottle Rum
1 bottle Brandy
juice of 9 Lemons
12 teaspoonfuls powdered
  sugar
1 bottle soda-water
  Use large punch bowl with
  block of ice. If desirable
  use boiling water and leave
  out the ice. Keep stirring
  and serve in small stem
  glasses. Decorate with
  slices of fruit in season

Punches

Sauternes Punch

lb. powdered sugar
quarts Sauternes
oz. Maraschino
oz. Curaçao
oz. Grand Marnier
Use punch bowl, a block of
ice, and add slices of fruit in
season

Tom and Jerry Punch

horoughly beat up yolks of
12 eggs
horoughly beat up whites of
12 eggs
horoughly mix the two
together adding
1 tablespoonful of
powdered sugar to each egg

horoughly mix the three ingredients together. Use large
unch bowl. Keep stirring so that sugar will not settle on
ottom of bowl. Use medium-size stem glass, china mug
ith handle or small tea-cup. Put 2 tablespoonsful of
tter in each cup. Add ½ measure Brandy and ½ measure
um. Fill with absolutely boiling water. Sprinkle nutmeg
top. Serve with spoon.

Prepared Punches
for bottling

There are tremendous advantages in having real Punch
bottled and ready to hand at any time. To accomplish this, it
is necessary to prepare the Punch in the form of a
concentrated essence, the addition of hot or cold water being
the only necessary step to produce a delicious Punch. Here
are some:

1½ gallons Arrack   *Essence of Arrack Punch*
3 gallons Spirits
3 gallons plain syrup
½ pint Tincture of Lemon
   Peel
   Mix all together and it is
   ready for immediate use

5 gallons Strong Brandy   *Essence of Brandy Punch*
3 gallons plain syrup
½ pint Tincture of Lemon
   Peel
½ pint Tincture of Orange
   Peel
3 oz. Tincture of All-spice
1 oz. Tincture of Cloves
   Mix the tinctures with the
   Brandy and add the syrup

Prepared Punches for Bottling

Essence of Claret Punch

5 gallons Claret
2½ gallons Spirits
3 gallons plain syrup
1 pint Tincture of Lemon Peel
½ pint Raspberry Juice
1 oz. Tartaric Acid
1½ oz. Tincture of Cloves
1½ oz. Tincture of Cinnamon

First dissolve the tartaric acid in a small portion of the Spirits. Mix the tinctures with the remainder of the Spirits. Pour the two mixtures together and add the remaining ingredients

Cups

Use small glass jug	*Cider Cup (No. 1)*
1 oz. Maraschino	*(4 people)*
1 oz. Curaçao	
1 oz. Brandy	
1 quart Cider	
4 lumps of ice	
Add 1 split of soda-water	
Stir gently and decorate with slices of fruit in season	

Use large glass jug	*Cider Cup (No. 2)*
1 oz. Apple Brandy	*(4 people)*
1 oz. Brandy	
1 oz. Orange Curaçao	
3 lumps of ice	
1 bottle Cider	
1 split of soda-water	
Decorate with slice of fruit add 2 sprigs of mint on top	

1 tablespoonful powdered sugar	*Champagne Cup*
2 oz. Brandy	
2 oz. Curaçao	
1 oz. Maraschino	
1 oz. Grand Marnier	
1 quart Champagne	
Serve in large pitcher with 4 lumps of ice, decorate with slices of orange and pineapple and 1 very small slice of cucumber peel 3 or 4 sprigs of fresh mint on top	

Cups

Claret Cup

1 oz. Maraschino
2 oz. Curaçao
2 tablespoonsful powdered
    sugar
1 quart Claret
    Serve in large jug with 4
    lumps of ice, decorate with
    slices of orange and
    pineapple and 1 very
    small slice of cucumber
    peel. Add 3 or 4 sprigs of
    fresh mint on top

Peach Cup

Carefully peel one or two fine ripe peaches and cut up with a
silver knife into small pieces, losing as little juice as possible,
then place into suitable Cup Vessel (glass bowl or soup
tureen).

Pour one bottle of light Still Moselle over the fruit and add
2 or 3 tablespoonsful of castor sugar. Stir the mixture gently
and cover over carefully, leaving it to draw for 20–30
minutes when another bottle of Still Moselle, previously iced,
should be added.

At the moment of serving, a bottle of Sparkling Moselle
should be added to the Cup, which should then be tasted
and, if necessary, further sugar added. Serve in suitable
glasses. It is advisable to keep the fruit back in the bowl.
The Cup should be carefully iced, *but on no account should ice be
put into the Cup*.

Cups

tablespoonful powdered
sugar
spirit measure Brandy
oz. Curaçao
oz. Maraschino
oz. Grand Marnier
quart Cider or Perry
Serve in large pitcher with
4 lumps of ice, decorate
with slices of orange and
pineapple and 1 very
small slice of cucumber
peel. Add 3 or 4 sprigs of
fresh mint on top

*Perry or Champagne
Cider Cup (No. 1)*

spirit measure Applejack
oz. Brandy
oz. Orange Curaçao
lumps of ice
bottle Cider or Perry
Serve in large pitcher and
decorate with slices of fruit
Add 2 sprigs of mint on top

*Perry or Champagne
Cider Cup (No. 2)*

oz. Maraschino
oz. Curaçao
tablespoonful sugar
quart Rhine wine
Serve in large jug with 4
lumps of ice. Decorate with
slices of orange and
pineapple and 1 very
small slice of cucumber
peel. Add 3 or 4 sprigs of
fresh mint on top

Rhine Wine Cup

Cups

Sauternes Cup   The same as for Rhine wine
Cup, substituting Sauternes
for the Rhine wine

After-Dinner Cocktails

½ Prunelle Brandy   *After Dinner Cocktail*
½ Cherry Brandy
4 dashes Lemon Juice
  Shake well and strain into
  sherry glass

½ Apricot Brandy   *After Supper Cocktail*
½ Curaçao
4 dashes Lemon Juice
  Shake well and strain into
  cocktail glass

⅓ Kirsch   *Albertine Cocktail*
⅓ Cointreau
⅓ Chartreuse
a few drops of Maraschino
  Shake well and strain into
  cocktail glass

½ Dry Gin   *Alexander Cocktail*
¼ Crème de Cacao   *(No. 1)*
¼ sweet cream
  Shake well and strain into
  cocktail glass

⅓ Crème de Cacao   *Alexander Cocktail*
⅓ Brandy   *(No. 2)*
⅓ fresh cream
  Shake well and strain into
  cocktail glass

After-Dinner Cocktails

Alexandra's Sister
Cocktail
⅓ Gin
⅓ cream
⅓ Crème de Menthe
Shake well and strain into
cocktail glass

Angel's Kiss Cocktail
¼ Crème de Cacao
¼ Prunelle Brandy
¼ Crème de Violette
¼ sweet cream
Use liqueur glass and pour
ingredients very carefully
so that they do not mix

Angel's Tip Cocktail
¾ Crème de Cacao
¼ fresh cream
Use liqueur glass and float
cream on top

Angel's Wing Cocktail
½ Crème de Cacao
½ Prunelle Brandy
Use liqueur glass and pour
ingredients very carefully
so that they do not mix.
Pour a little sweet cream on
top

Babbie's Special Cocktail
1 dash Gin
⅓ sweet cream
⅔ Apricot Brandy
Shake well and strain into
cocktail glass

After-Dinner Cocktails

Barbara Cocktail

fresh cream
Crème de Cacao
Vodka
Shake well and strain into
cocktail glass

Buds Special Cocktail

dash Angostura Bitters
sweet cream
Cointreau
Shake well and strain into
cocktail glass

Ethel Cocktail

Apricot Brandy
White Crème de Menthe
Curaçao
Shake well and strain into
cocktail glass

Fifth Avenue Cocktail

Crème de Cacao
Apricot Brandy
sweet cream
Use liqueur glass and pour
carefully so that ingredients
do not mix

Prince's Smile Cocktail

dash Lemon Juice
Apricot Brandy
Apple Brandy
Dry Gin
Shake well and strain into
cocktail glass

After-Dinner Cocktails

Princess Cocktail
- ¾ Apricot Brandy
- ¼ sweet cream
  Use liqueur glass and pour cream carefully so that it does not mix

Quelle Vie Cocktail
- ⅓ Kummel
- ⅔ Brandy
  Stir well and strain into cocktail glass

Rainbow Cocktail
- ⅐ Crème de Cacao
- ⅐ Crème de Violette
- ⅐ Yellow Chartreuse
- ⅐ Maraschino
- ⅐ Bénédictine
- ⅐ Green Chartreuse
- ⅐ Brandy
  Use liqueur glass and pour ingredients very carefully so that they do not mix

Savoy Cocktail
- ⅓ Crème de Cacao
- ⅓ Bénédictine
- ⅓ Brandy
  Use liqueur glass and pour ingredients carefully so that they do not mix

Stars and Stripes Cocktail
- ⅓ Crème de Cassis
- ⅓ Maraschino
- ⅓ Green Chartreuse
  Use liqueur glass and pour ingredients carefully so that they do not mix

After-Dinner Cocktails

White Crème de Menthe   *Stinger Cocktail*
Brandy
Shake well and strain into
cocktail glass

Grenadine   *Sunrise Cocktail*
Crème de Violette
Yellow Chartreuse
Cointreau
Use liqueur glass and pour
ingredients carefully so that
they do not mix

Yellow Chartreuse   *Three-quarter Back*
Curaçao   *Cocktail*
Brandy
Use liqueur glass and pour
ingredients carefully so that
they do not mix

Grenadine   *Union Jack Cocktail*
Maraschino
Green Chartreuse
Use liqueur glass and pour
ingredients carefully so that
they do not mix

Reviver Cocktails

¾ Sweet Vermouth
¼ Fernet Branca
  Shake and strain into
  cocktail glass

Baraccas Cocktail

¼ Sweet Vermouth
¼ Apple Brandy
½ Brandy
  Shake well and strain into
  cocktail glass

Corpse Reviver Cocktail
(No. 1)

¼ Lemon Juice
¼ Lillet
¼ Cointreau
¼ Dry Gin
1 dash Absinthe
  Shake well and strain into
  cocktail glass

Corpse Reviver Cocktail
(No. 2)

yolk of 1 fresh egg
1 teaspoonful powdered sugar
2 dashes Absinthe
2 dashes Curaçao
2 dashes Crème de Noyau
1 oz. Rum
  Shake well and strain into
  cocktail glass

Eye-Opener Cocktail

1 teaspoonful Grenadine
2 oz. Brandy
juice of ½ Lemon
  Shake well and strain into
  medium-size wineglass. Fill
  up with Champagne

Harry's Pick-Me-Up
Cocktail

Reviver Cocktails

I.B.F. Pick-Me-Up Cocktail

In a wineglass place 1 lump of ice, 3 dashes of Fernet Branca, 3 dashes of Curaçao, and 1 oz. of Brandy. Fill up with Champagne
Stir and squeeze lemon peel on top

Morning After Cocktail

1 egg
1 teaspoonful Worcestershire Sauce
Do not break the egg

Prairie Hen Cocktail

2 dashes vinegar
1 teaspoonful Worcestershire Sauce
1 egg
2 dashes Tabasco Sauce
a little pepper and salt
Do not break the egg

Prairie Oyster Cocktail

2 dashes vinegar
yolk of 1 egg
1 teaspoonful Worcestershire Sauce
1 teaspoonful Tomato Ketchup
a dash of pepper on top
Do not break the yolk of the egg

Reviver Cocktails

⅓ Brandy
⅓ Fernet Branca
⅓ White Crème de Menthe
Shake and strain into
cocktail glass

*Savoy Corpse Reviver
Cocktail*

dashes Angostura Bitters
Fernet Branca
Brandy
Shake well and strain into
cocktail glass

Stomach Reviver Cocktail

Glossary

ABRICOTINE: A French apricot brandy. Colour: bright tawny. Apricot and cognac.

ABSINTHE: A highly concentrated wormwood distillate.

ADVOCAAT: A Dutch liqueur. Flavour: eggs and brandy.

AMER PICON: A bitter liqueur-wine. An aperitif.

ANGOSTURA: A brand of "Bitters" made at Port of Spain, Trinidad. Rum base and aromatic herbs and roots.

ANISETTE: A liqueur. Flavour: aniseed.

APPLE BRANDY: Distilled cider. A potable spirit, unsweetened.

APRICOT BRANDY: Flavour: apricot and brandy.

AQUAVIT: A strong, colourless spirit.

ARMAGNAC: Brandy distilled from wine from the Bas-Armagnac.

ARRACK: A spirituous liqueur distilled from rice and sugar-cane, flavoured with Eastern fruits and roots.

AURIUM: An orange-flavoured liqueur from Pineta di Pescara (Italy).

BÉNÉDICTINE: A popular liqueur distilled by the monks at Fécamp (France). Known as D.O.M.

BISHOP: Port and sugar made hot with cloves and with an orange steeped in it.

BYRRH: A French aperitif.

CALORIC: A punch made and bottled in Sweden.

CALVADOS: A fine distilled apple brandy.

CAMPARI BITTERS: Extract of Capsicum. A very fine bitters.

CAPERITIF: An aperitif from the Cape.

CASSIS: A liqueur. Flavour: black currants.

CHARTREUSE: A sweet liqueur, yellow or green. A secret recipe. Made originally by monks in France: now made in Spain.

COGNAC: Brandy distilled from wine made in the Charente district of France.

Glossary

COINTREAU: A trebly-distilled liqueur.

CORDIAL MÉDOC: Similar to distilled claret.

CRÈME DE CACAO: A French liqueur with a flavour of cocoa.

CRÈME DE CIEL: A Dutch liqueur similar to Curaçao.

CRÈME DE MENTHE: A white or green liqueur made of wine or grain spirit. Flavour: peppermint.

CRÈME YVETTE: An American liqueur. Flavour: violets.

CURAÇAO: A liqueur made of wine or grain spirit and orange peel.

DANZIGER GOLDWASSER: A sweet liqueur with flakes of gold leaf. Flavour: aniseed and orange.

DANZIGER SILBERWASSER: A liqueur with flakes of silver leaf. Flavour: aniseed and orange.

DRAMBUIE: A Scotch liqueur. Flavour of Scotch whisky and honey.

DUBONNET: A French tonic with a quinine taste. An aperitif.

FERNET BRANCA: An Italian bitters. One of the principal ingredients is logwood from Bolivia.

FORBIDDEN FRUIT: An American liqueur. Sweet and bitter. Flavour: grapefruit and orange.

GRENADINE: A very sweet syrup flavoured with pomegranate juice.

KIRSCHWASSER: A liqueur distilled with the kernels of cherry stones.

LILLET: An aperitif made with white wine fortified with Armagnac.

MARASCHINO: A liqueur from Zara in Dalmatia. Flavour: cherries.

MUST: Grape juice before it has fermented.

NOYAU: A sweetened liqueur flavoured with almond kernels.

OXYGENÉE: Similar to Absinthe.

Glossary

PASSION FRUIT: A sterilized juice extract of passion
fruit from Australia, New Zealand and South Africa.

PEYCHAUD BITTERS: An aromatic bitters from
America.

SAKÉ: A spirit distilled from rice.

SCHNAPPS: A very strong spirit of the gin type, widely
favoured in Germany, Holland, Scandinavia, etc.

SLOE GIN: Gin in which sloe-berries have been steeped.

TABASCO: A very hot extract of red pepper.

TEQUILA: An aperitif: a spirit distilled from a Mexican
cactus.

VAN DER HUM: A liqueur made in South Africa.
Flavour: tangerine.

VERMOUTH (Dry): A white wine with an infusion of
camomile flowers.

VERMOUTH (Sweet): A white wine with an infusion of
various aromatic herbs.

VODKA: A spirit distillation of grain or potatoes.